The Cotswol
Compani...

An Insider Guide
2nd Edition

Cotswold Way National Trail

Broadway
Chipping Campden
Stanton
Wood Stanway
Winchcombe
Cleeve Hill
Prestbury Hill
Cheltenham
Leckampton Hill
Seven Springs
Birdlip
Painswick
Stroud
King's Stanley
Dursley
Wotton under Edge
Hawkesbury Upton
Old Sodbury
Tormarton
Cold Ashton
Bath

Cotswolds National Landscape

Cotswold Way Association

Edited by Keith Sisson

The Cotswold Way Association

The Cotswold Way Association (CWA) is a Charitable Incorporated Organisation registered with the UK Charity Commission. It's an 'open' membership charity, which means anyone can join and contribute to its activities if they share its mission. This is 'To promote the conservation and protection of the Cotswold Way National Trail and the surrounding environment of the Cotswold Way National Trail and its habitats (including the Cotswold Way Circular Walks, linking and access routes and other named trails in the area) for the public benefit'.

eBook first published in 2022; this second edition published in 2024
eBook ISBN: 978-1-7398416-2-1

Paperback first published in 2022; this second edition published in 2024
Paperback ISBN: 978-1-7398416-3-8

Both are available from **www.cotswoldwayassociation.org.uk**

Printed and bound by CPI Group (UK) Ltd, Croydon, CR0 4YY

www.cotswoldwayassociation.org.uk

Contents

Acknowledgements

There isn't enough space to name all the people who helped to make this book possible. Some do deserve to be so recognised, though. These include the five people who made up what might be described as the 'editorial team'. John Bartam, Steve Holbrow, Malcolm Higgins, Margaret Reid and Keith Sisson. As well as being Trustees, three of these had roles with the CWA: John was chair, Malcolm Secretary and Keith editor of its *Cotswold WayMarker* newsletter. Margaret and Steve were very active CWA members and 'volunteers', Margaret looking after membership as well as being Head Cotswold Voluntary Warden at the time and Steve helping with social media.

Getting from A to B involved a three-stage process: Keith turning into rough chapter drafts the notes of the Cotswold Voluntary Wardens who'd led the annual Cotswold Way walks pre-Covid-19; his four colleagues helping to knock the chapters into shape for wider reading and comment; and two further groups of Cotswold Wardens adding corrections and suggestions for improvement, along with any quirky anecdotes and stories that would help to put a smile on people's faces. These were the coordinators of the Wardens who regularly patrol a stretch of the trail and the stage leaders of the relay walk held in September 2021 to celebrate the delayed Cotswold Way 50th anniversary. It's with some justification, therefore, that 'An Insider Guide' is the book's subtitle.

In this second edition Keith has done some updating. Chapter 11, for example, reminds us that Winchcombe has yet another claim to fame: on 28 February 2021 it was the landing point of one of the largest meteorites ever to have hit the UK. His main aim, however, has been to correct the first edition's typographical errors and rephrase its sections needing to be clearer. Keith is especially grateful to Peter and June Clements for their painstaking efforts in helping to highlight these.

Also to be emphasised is that the book's not just a matter of text. It also has many images, with special thanks due to the following:
- Rob Talbot for the National Tail maps in these preliminaries and chapters 1 and 2
- Bob Child for the specially designed stage maps in chapters 3-12
- Mark Richards for allowing his pen & ink drawings to grace the book throughout
- Mike Cripps, Richard Wilson, Harvey Mattinson, Jean Booth and Rob Talbot for individual photographs in Chapters 3, 4, 9, 10 and 12 respectively.

As far as the editorial team have been able to establish, the other images appearing in the book are in the public domain either on websites or in general publications. Unless posted otherwise at the foot of the image, their source is the CWA itself and/or the Cotswold National Landscape (CNL). As already indicated, in the few cases where this is not the case, every effort has been made to attribute the source properly, bearing in mind all these images are in the public domain. Any mistakes drawn to the CWA's attention will be rectified at the earliest opportunity.

A word about the sources for the text is also appropriate. A starting point for many of the original walk leader notes was **Wikipedia**. As the many references in the text suggest, these were double checked, retained and developed along with links in the eBook. There are very good reasons. Wikipedia is not only a valuable source of information in itself, but also an excellent link to further sources, including coverage of any differences of opinion and interpretation. In a publication like this, referring to Wikipedia also means not having to spell out the article details, book references and page numbers expected in an academic work. It's similarly possible to dispense with footnotes in the interest of text flow and readability. If you want, you can follow up the links in the eBook edition.

The publications of bodies such as the Cotswold National Landscape, English Heritage (for the **Great Witcombe Roman Villa**), Natural England, National Trails and the National Trust (especially for **Crickley Country Park**, **Dyrham Park** and **Haresfield Beacon**) were another valuable source of information on specific features in both the original notes and the final book. The same is true of the websites of organisations responsible for the **Broadway Tower**, **Cleeve Common**, **Prinknash Abbey**, the **Stanway Estate**, **Stinchcombe Hill** and **Sudeley Castle**.

The Cotswold Way is also blessed because the towns through which it runs have active local history societies and/or heritage centres. As their websites confirm, these proved to be a rich source of detailed historical information used in preparing the final text. Again in alphabetical order, with links to their websites in the eBook, they are:

Broadway

Chipping Campden

Dursley & Cam

Painswick

Winchcombe

Wotton-under-Edge

In the case of designated and scheduled sites, the book is especially indebted to **Historic England**. Such is the quality of the entries, it rarely made sense to try to offer a summary, explaining why many of its descriptions are quoted in full. Also very helpful, particularly in the case of barrows and hillforts, was Tim Copeland's *Archaeological Walking Guide to the Cotswold Way*.

Last but by no means least, Mark Richard's *The Cotswold Way. The complete walker's guide* deserves a special mention. Not only is it the home of the wonderful original pen and ink drawings that he very generously allowed us to use. The book proved to be a great reference point for double checking to make sure nothing important had been left out!

Foreword by Mark Richards
… ever forward with the winding trail

My outward view of the world derives from an upbringing as a Cotswold farmer. The first forty years indeed spent tilling the heavy Lias clay and rearing Hereford cattle in the Evenlode valley. My recreation was always country walking, so in 1969 seeking adventure I moved from Moreton-in-Marsh Young Farmers' Club to Gloucestershire Mountaineering Club, where I met Tony Drake - one of the architects of the Cotswold Way.

My love of pen & ink drawing, nurtured by Alfred Wainwright, prompted Tony to suggest I create the very first guide to The Cotswold Way. The newly launched trail was in need of its own 'Wainwright' guide. Major Clarke had prepared a 10-page A4 stapled description for walkers to find the nascent route and that was my guide too. What fun I had. Quirkily I did not begin at the start, stepping into its midst walking from Duckpool Street in Winchcombe up to Belas Knap via Wadfield to get a feel for the journey. Ironically a section of the original route that recently has been the subject of some controversy. Over the years as an author/artist I have revisited the route creating three distinct walking guides, the original 1973 Thornhill Press booklet, a Penguin Books paperback in 1984 and the Reardon guide published in 1995.

For all that I now live in Cumbria the route remains dear to my heart, so it was wonderful news when it gained National Trail status. The trail has many fans, with volunteers helping to maintain it supported by an enthusiastic Cotswold Way Association. All breathe renewed life into the care of the route and an appreciation of the gorgeous scarp landscape through which it skips. As the seasons unfold you will always find pleasure and invigoration through constantly changing perspectives up and down the wooded escarpment, across fields and commons, most notably north and west across the spreading Evesham and Severn vales. The villages and towns, built with a warm-toned stone, imbue any walk with a lasting glow. Here's to the next fifty years of 'Cotsaller's' delight dawning fresh each new day.

Mark Richards
markrichardswalking.co.uk
October 2021

Pen and ink drawings throughout - by kind permission of Mark Richards

Chapter 1
About this book

This book is about the Cotswold Way. One of the UK's sixteen designated national trails, it's internationally renowned and attracts walkers from all over the world. What it might lack in length or difficulty - it's just 102 miles long (162kms) and doesn't rise much above 330 metres - it more than makes up for in beauty and interest. It follows a dramatic limestone escarpment linking the Georgian city of Bath in the south to the medieval market town of Chipping Campden in the north. In doing so, it passes through quintessential English countryside dotted with small towns, villages and ancient monuments.

The trail is also pretty accessible. Bath is just 18 miles or 29 kms from Bristol international airport and Chipping Campden 35 miles (56 kms) from Birmingham's. London Heathrow is some two hours away.

The main route of the present day Cotswold Way was the brainchild of walkers from the Gloucestershire and South Gloucestershire Ramblers groups - notably Tony Drake and Cyril Trenfield respectively. It was first mooted some seventy years ago following the passing of the National Parks and Access to the Countryside Act of 1949 providing for the creation of long distance paths. It was only in 1968, however, that things really began to move, with Gloucestershire County Council preparing the route based on existing local public rights of way. The Cotswold Way was formally launched in May 1970 and became a designated National Trail in May 2007. Fittingly, there are memorials to both Tony and Cyril on the trail: Tony's is a special waymark post near Painswick (see Chapter 8) and Cyril's a recently restored and CWA-funded bench near Dyrham Park.

CYRIL TRENFIELD (1928-2007)
A LIFE DEDICATED TO THE COUNTRYSIDE AND THE COTSWOLD WAY

A team effort

Hardly surprisingly, the Cotswold Way has spawned lots of books, with the internet bringing a proliferation of walkers' blogs more recently. This is because, as Chapter 2 explains in greater detail, its 102 miles offer something for every grade of walker, with a unique landscape, marvellous views of the surrounding countryside, glimpses of wonderful wildlife and passage through small towns and villages steeped in history.

This book is nonetheless very distinctive. As in the case of the Cotswolds Way's route, its outstanding feature is that it builds on the contributions of a great many people with very special knowledge and experience of walking the trail. Especially notable are the contributions of three groups of Cotswold Voluntary Wardens, helping to explain why 'an insider guide' is the sub-title.

One group comprises those who have led stretches of the Cotswold Way guided walks the Wardens offer. It's their pre-Covid-19 notes, last used in 2019, that form the basis of Chapters 3 to 12 of the book.

The acorn beckons

The involvement of the second and third groups is more recent. The second comprises the Cotswold Way Wardens who are responsible for regularly patrolling a stretch of the trail and the third those who led stages of the relay walk held to celebrate the (covid-postponed) 50th anniversary of the Cotswold Way in 2021. At the time of the relay, in September 2021, both groups not only generously read and commented on draft chapters, but also added suggestions for improvement, along with quirky anecdotes and stories that would help to put a smile on people's faces. The final outcome, therefore, is the product of the knowledge and experience of a great many people who know and love the Cotswold Way.

The book's aims

This book also has very distinctive aims. Yes, it has maps to help you put things into perspective. But, no, they're not designed to give you step by step directions - follow the many well-positioned waymarks to follow the route and take an Ordnance Survey map as you would for any serious walking in the UK. In a nutshell, as well as extolling the unique virtues of the trail and explaining why it's a 'must do' walk, the main aim is to help you get the very most out of the walk - to give you an idea of the main points of interest to look out for, where to get the best views and take photographs, and so on. If you hadn't thought about stepping out on the Cotswold Way, hopefully you will after reading it. If you've decided to walk the trail, or just a section or sections - perhaps one of its Circular Walks - it will add considerably to your anticipation and enjoyment. If you've already walked on the trail, it will help you to remember the good times you had and, perhaps, whet your appetite to come back to see what you missed.

A second aim, let's not beat around the bush, is to raise money towards the upkeep and improvement of the trail. You might wonder why money is a problem given that the Cotswold Way is a national trail. The simple answer, put bluntly, is that austerity and budget cuts mean that the grant provided by the national government through Natural England is insufficient. A 'Trail Partnership' embracing local authorities is responsible for the path on the ground and keeping it up to the high standards set for National Trails. Trouble is local authorities don't have the wherewithal to make up the difference.

It was in the expectation that things were unlikely to change that, in 2016, a small group of Cotswolds Wardens and Ramblers agreed to take action in their personal capacities. Briefly put, they decided to follow the example of the Friends of the Ridgeway and South West Coast Path Association and set up the Cotswold Way Association (CWA). As already indicated, the CWA is a Charitable Incorporated Organisation registered with the UK Charity Commission: an 'open' membership charity, which anyone can join and contribute to.

Because the challenge of conserving this much loved trail for future generations to enjoy is pretty immense. The restoration and renewal that the CWA funds is more or less a continuous process involving very practical projects such as:

- better waymarking
- supplying information boards
- installing benches (only where appropriate)
- creating steps and installing handrails on steep slopes
- replacing stiles with gates
- installing boardwalks
- tackling erosion

You'll find recent examples of improvement in the illustrations at the end of the chapter.

If you're wondering why erosion is such a problem, remember that the Cotswold Way's popularity attracts some 200,000 walkers a year, causing significant damage to the trail's surface. This is especially true at pinch-points such as stiles and kissing gates. Also, it isn't enough just to put down hardcore or a bundle of stones if you are trying to look after a fantastic National Trail in a lovely national landscape with complicated geology. For a significant part of the route, the subsoil below the spring line is soft clays. These 'puddle' wonderfully under walkers' feet, forming a soft, deep, watertight soup into which any amount of stone seems to disappear in a matter of months - it really is a case of pouring money down the drain!

As the illustrations at the Chapter's end show, Cotswold Warden experiments have suggested the best solution is to install a layer of geotext material to help prevent the base being washed away, along with honeycomb ecogrid to hold the stone, followed by a topping. Digging a 'french' drain also helps.

It goes without saying that considerable and ongoing resources are required to look after a national treasure like the Cotswold Way. The material costs of restoring ten metres of trail from erosion add up to £300. Those of a three metre boardwalk are around £200 and a kissing gate about £400 plus £75 in materials to make good the area around it - and the Cotswold Way has a couple of hundred or so. If commercial contractors are used on these jobs instead of volunteers, these costs can be more than doubled.

Some projects can run into thousands of pounds. As you'll see from the photographs at the end of Chapter 9, one such is on Leckhampton Hill above Cheltenham. The project, which was completed in September 2021 with the generous support of the HF Holidays Pathways Fund, now allows ALL users to have access to the hill's escarpment. Practically, it involved re-ramping, smoothing and grading a 2-3 metre wide path on both sides of a gate virtually impassable by a wheelchair or pushchair. Logistically, it meant having to deliver to the site some 150 tonnes of limestone dust and Cotswold stone.

There is a third reason for publishing the book. It is to encourage you, if you can, to become involved in activities supporting the Cotswold Way and other footpaths in the Cotswolds. You could become a member or volunteer or Trustee with the CWA. You could become a Cotswold Warden, patrolling parish footpaths or leading walks or joining one of their regular work parties - an outdoor gym with all-round advantages over the indoor variety even if it will sometimes feel as if you're digging holes just to fill them in!

You can also make a donation, organise a fundraising event on behalf of the CWA or sponsor someone taking part in such an event. You'll find further details of how to do these if you go to the Cotswold Way Association website.

Several options

When thinking about walking the Cotswold Way, people are often given the impression they have just two options: you walk north-south or south-north. Both directions have their supporters. Advocates of south-north reckon it gets better and more exciting the further north you go. Those who say north-south disagree and point to the benefit of walking into rather than out of the Georgian city of Bath.

There's never likely to be a consensus about the direction to walk the Cotswold Way. It's a magnificent walk whether you walk N-S from Chipping Campden to Bath or S-N the other way. And if it's something that bugs you, why not do it both ways for different experiences?

Either way, you don't have to walk the trail from end to end in one go. You can sign up for an organised walk along it with the Cotswold Voluntary Wardens in ten monthly day walks. You can leave your car at Winchcombe or Cold Ashton near Bath and then a bus will take you to the start of each stage of the walk and return you back at the end of the day. The Cotswold Way Association website has the details.

You can also consider walking the trail in bite sized segments independently. One of the CWA Trustees, Harvey Mattinson, breaks it down into sixteen 6-7 mile sections based on available parking.

Again, you'll find details of his Cotswold Way in Stages on the CWA website.

If your main interest is to make the most of what it has to offer rather than being fussed about 'doing' the Cotswold Way, there's a serious alternative to an 'end-to-end' approach. It is to follow in the footsteps of what more and more walkers are taking: it is to target the impressive network of Cotswold Way Circular Walks along the 102 mile route. As you will see from the map below, there are no fewer than twelve such walks, plus two friendship trails, all hugely popular. Putting your energies into these walks means you will be able to focus on the very best that the trail has to offer. You can download maps of all the Cotswold Way Circular Walks from the National Trails website. There are also brief details of the walks at the end of the relevant stage chapters in this book.

The National Trail website also has a few suggested itineraries for those who do not have the time to walk the whole trail. Some of these are organised by walking companies. Cotswold Walks and Hike & Bikes, who are business members of the CWA, can be recommended.

You might also like to know that the Cotswold Voluntary Wardens run a regular programme of shorter guided walks across the Cotswolds, many of which will involve sections of the national trail. Typically, they are between four and ten miles and will introduce you to the very best the Cotswolds have to offer. You'll find details in the *Cotswold Lion* free magazine published twice a year and available in TICs, libraries, hotels, shops and many other outlets. Alternatively, visit the Cotswold National Landscape website for it.

Cotswold Way National Trail

Cotswolds National Landscape

Cotswold Way Circular Walks
1 Chipping Campden
2 Broadway nd Tower
3 Stanton/Snowshill
4 Winchcombe - Belas Knap
5 Cleeve Hill
6 Leckhampton Hill
7 Cranham Woods
8 Selsey
9 Cam Long Down and Uley
10 Wotton Under Edge
11 Old Sodbury
12 Journey's End - Bath
KFT Stinchcombe Hill
BFT Haresfield Beacon

Practical information

The National Trail Website is the best place to start for practical information. It has an interactive map covering the trail, including a distance measurer, points of interest, accommodation and services. Answers are given to various questions and a GPX file of the trail can be downloaded. The Cotswold National Landscape website provides loads of information on the Cotswolds and how to explore this valuable protected landscape. If you would like to whet your appetite for walking the trail or need to check on a few locations, then why not try the Cotswold National Trail on Google Street View to be found there. It's a bit clunky but is worth a look.

If you are looking for a traditional directions-giving guide, the following are currently available from either the National Trails Shop or other retailers:

- **Cotswold Way** by Anthony Burton. This is the official national trail guidebook and provides route details and general information on points of interest. It's written from north to south.
- **Walking the Cotswold Way** by Kev Reynolds. This is a Cicerone guide and also covers the route and general information. It's written in both directions. Latest edition (2021) has up-to-date information on accommodation.
- **Cotswold Way Trailblazer Guide** by Tricia & Bob Hayne and Henry Stedman. In addition to detailed route information this also provides reasonably up to date information on services as well as accommodation. It's written from north to south.

Also valuable are:

- **Archaeological Walking Guide to the Cotswold Way** by Tim Copeland. This is a specialist guidebook which focuses on the trail's historical features.
- **Slow Travel - The Cotswolds** by Caroline Mills. This is an excellent general guide to the Cotswolds with lots of suggestions for places to visit off the normal tourist routes.

As luck would have it, at the beginning of October 2021, just as the first edition was being finalised, Historic England announced that, for the first time, it was making freely available online the results of over 30 years of aerial photograph mapping projects involving over 500,000 aerial photographs.

Here are details of those covering the Cotswold Way:
- **An Archaeological Survey in the Severn Vale, Gloucestershire: A Highlight Report for the National Mapping Programme NMP**
- **An Archaeological Aerial Photograph Interpretation in the Cotswold Hills: A Report for the National Mapping Programme**
- **The North Cotswolds: A Highlight Report for the National Mapping Programme**

As for current maps, the Cotswold Way is marked on the 1:50,000 Landranger OS maps (sheet numbers N-S -151, 163, 162 and 172) and the 1:25,000 Explorer OS maps (sheet numbers from N to S - 205, OL45, 179, 168, 167 and 155). The Cotswold Way Harvey Map is particularly useful as it is a strip map on one sheet covering the whole trail and the Cotswold Way. A-Z Adventure Atlas also has the whole trail at 1:25,000 in book format. Both are available from the National Trails Shop.

If you're opting for the end-to-end approach, your No 1 priority is to book your accommodation in advance as places to stay are limited on some sections. *Walking the Cotswold Way* and the *Cotswold Way Trailblazer Guide* are your best sources of information. In addition to detailed route information, they offer a wealth of reasonably up to date information on accommodation and where to eat and drink along the trail, including local public transport arrangements. You can also check on their website for any significant changes. If you are looking for a place to stay which is an easy day's walk from Bath, Hill Farm, a business member of the CWA in Cold Ashton, is to be recommended.

The good news is that you don't have to carry a heavy pack to walk the Cotswold Way. Luggage transfer is available through several companies listed on the National Trails website. One of them is Cotswold Walkers Transport Services, which is a business member of the CWA. They will also handle taxi transfers along the trail. You'll find direct links to the most important sources of information about the practicalities in the e-book version.

For those thinking of any of the 'Cotswold Way in Stages' approaches, your priority is to plan your parking. This is something the traditional guides very rarely mention. In this case, you'll find suggestions at the end of each of the ten stage chapters. You're strongly recommended to have a couple in mind, just in case you pick the wrong day for your first choice!

One final thing. The Cotswold Way is a proper walk. Please treat it with the respect it deserves. Don't see it as just a challenge to be walked in quick time. Wear proper footwear and clothing. Take a walking pole for balance - the trail can get slippery when it's been raining - and a phone in case of emergencies. Carry plenty of liquid, especially in hot summer, to keep you hydrated.

The rest of the book

At the end of this chapter, you'll find illustrations of the types of improvement being funded by the CWA including gates, seats, notice boards, handrails and steps, along with an impression of what's involved in tackling erosion. The next chapter gives you background information on the Cotswolds that are the setting for the Cotswold Way - in particular, their geology, grasslands and woodland, settlement pattern, distinctive architecture and footpath network. There follow ten chapters each dealing with one of the typically ten mile or so stages that feature on the Cotswold Way walks led by Cotswold Wardens every year. Most walkers should find the ten miles or so achievable in a day. The sequence, South-North, is in line with Mark Richards' original The Cotswold Way and the editor's own experience of walking the trail. The parking information will also enable you to adjust the stages to suit - for example, if you want to spend more time in places like Winchcombe or Broadway.

You'll see that each of the stage chapters highlights a major theme, as well as drawing attention to the main points of interest, of attraction and of beauty, and of views. You will also find anecdotes, quirky stories and points of detail that will help you to gain a deeper appreciation than is normally possible (e.g. how the man responsible for building Dyrham House came up with the wherewithal, why J.K. Rowling so named the Dursley family in her Harry Potter books, how it is that a 'Cromwell's Stone' turns up in the middle of nowhere above Painswick, and why the Stanway Estate has strong connections with characters as different as Thomas á Becket and Peter Pan).

To enable you to put the trail into perspective and highlight the features close to it, each stage chapter includes a map drawn by Bob Child, a graphic designer whose Pear Tree Studios are based in the Cotswolds. Included, too, are copies of some of Mark Richard's wonderful original pen and ink drawings that first appeared in his The Cotswold Way. The complete walker's guide nearly forty years ago. As well as being gems in their own right, they help to remind us of that great tradition of walk books that Alfred Wainwright began with his famous introductions to the Lake District's fells.

A wooden kissing gate at Stumps Cross near Stanway

A restored seat near Dyrham originally installed in 1977

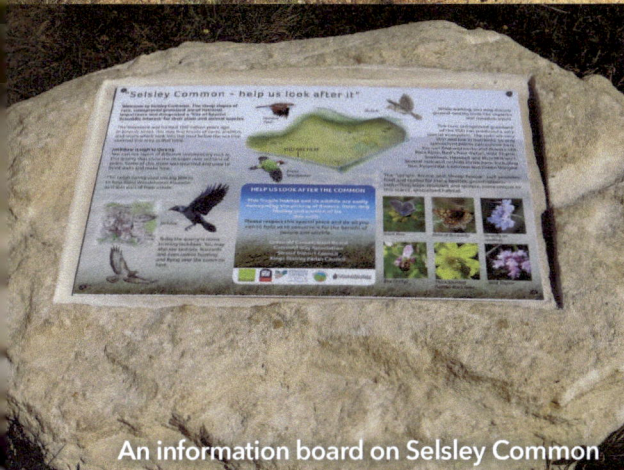

An information board on Selsley Common

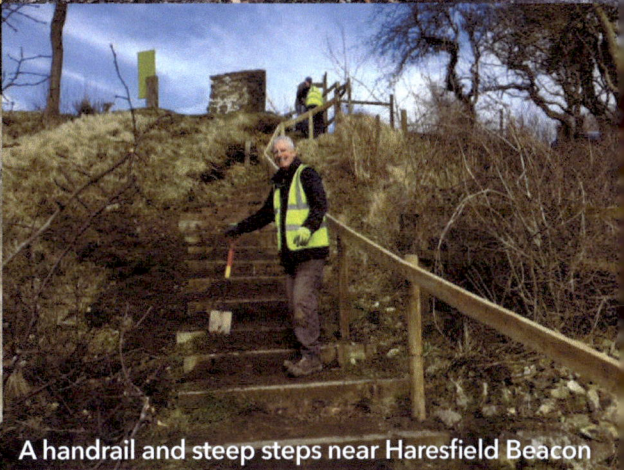

A handrail and steep steps near Haresfield Beacon

A 45 metre long handrail on a slippery slope near Weston

Tackling erosion - start with a 'french' drain

Install geotex and ecogrid

Make ready for topping

Chapter 2
The Cotswolds: a very special landscape

Most people will have a rough idea about the location of the Cotswolds that are home to the Cotswold Way. It's an area in south-central, West Midlands and south west England comprising the Cotswold Hills. They may not know, though, that there's an official definition. It comes in the form of the boundaries of the *Cotswolds National Landscape* (previously Area of Outstanding National Beauty or, to use the shorthand, AONB). As you'll see from the map below, it covers an area much larger than the county of Gloucestershire with which the Cotswolds are very often associated. Areas of Oxfordshire, Somerset, Warwickshire, Wiltshire and Worcestershire are also embraced - once upon time, more of which in Chapter 11, there was even a Winchcombshire. Altogether, the designated Cotswolds covers 787 square miles (2,040 km2) and is the third largest protected landscape in England after the Lake District and Yorkshire Dales national parks. Roughly eighty percent is farmland.

So what is it that makes the Cotswolds so special? The debate about the origin of the name gives us an inkling. According to the entry in Wikipedia, the name 'Cotswolds' is popularly understood to mean 'sheep enclosure in rolling hillsides' and incorporates the German word 'wald' meaning 'forest'. However, the Oxford *A Dictionary of British place names* has for many years accepted that the term Cotswold is derived from the 12th century word *Codesuualt*. Roughly this translates into 'Cod's-wold' or 'Cod's high open land', recognising over the years the meaning of 'wald' changed from 'forest' to 'open high ground'.

A much more comprehensive answer is to be found in Natural England's (NCA) so-called 'national area character area profile' for the Cotswolds. One of Natural England's responsibilities going back to various government strategy papers, such as *Biodiversity 2020*, and the *European Landscape Convention,* is to maintain profiles of areas that share similar landscape characteristics and follow natural lines in the landscape rather than administrative boundaries. There are 159 of them altogether and the Cotswolds are No 107. The NCA profile for the Cotswolds is especially valuable for two reasons: it helps us to identify the objective characteristics of the landscape with some authority; and, perhaps even more importantly, it enables us to appreciate how interdependent and mutually reinforcing the natural and built environments have become. Here, then, are the key characteristics or attributes associated with the Cotswolds drawing on the NCA profile.

A dramatic limestone escarpment

The key feature of the Cotswolds, the NCA profile suggests, is 'a dramatic limestone scarp'. Sometimes known locally as the 'edge', as in 'Wotton-under-Edge' near Stroud and 'Weston-sub-edge' near Chipping Campden, it rises above adjacent lowlands with dip (gradual) slopes, and steep combes, along with outliers illustrating the slow erosion of escarpments. Bredon Hill is one example of an outlier, helping to explain why the CNL boundary in the north west extends into Worcestershire; others are Brailes Hill and Castle Hill in South Warwickshire and Cam Long Down near Dursley, which you'll meet in Chapter 7. The limestone geology has formed the scarp and dip slope of the landscape, which in turn has influenced drainage, soils, vegetation, land use and settlement.

Coverage of the Cotswold National Landscape

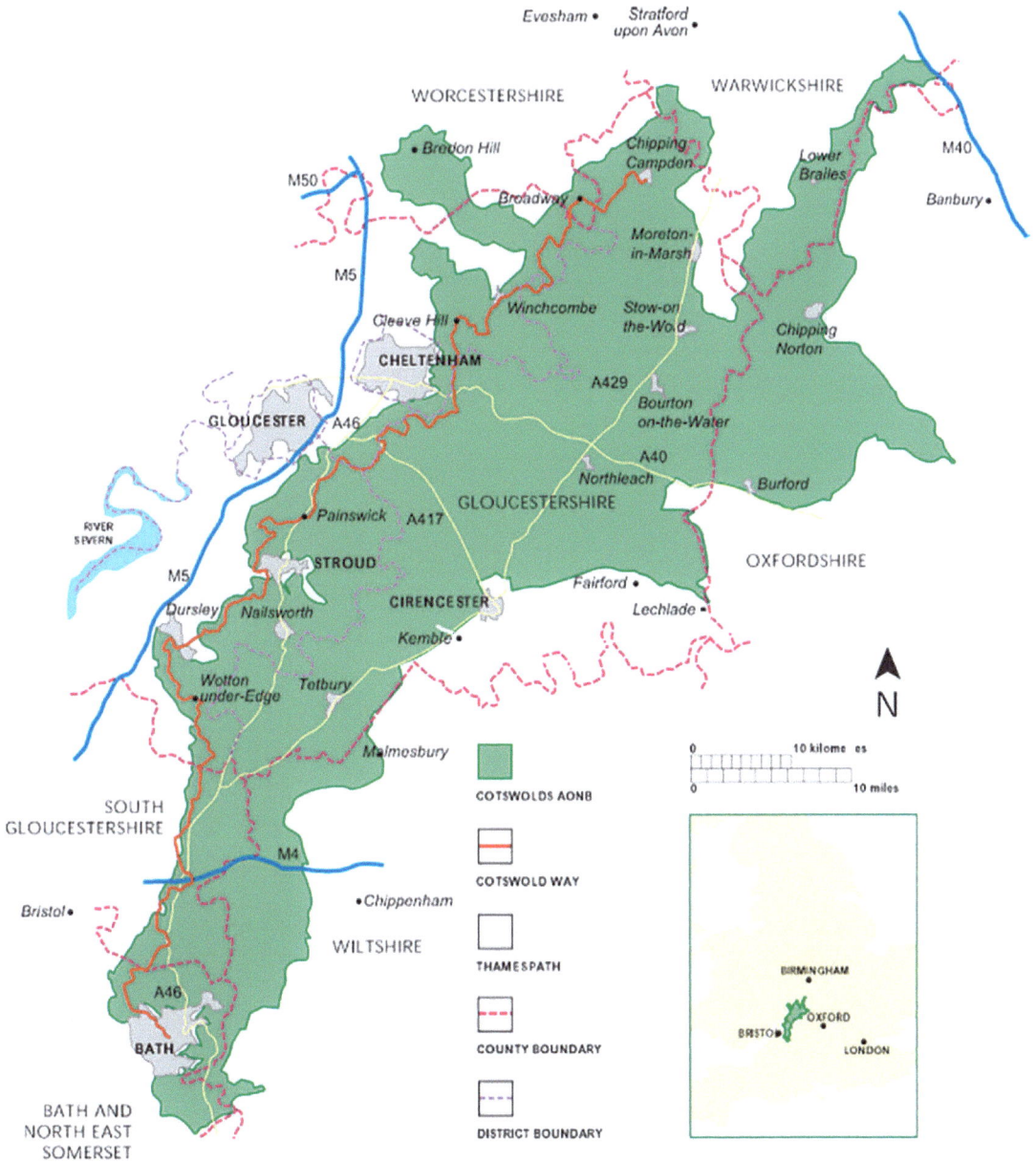

Geologists tell us that the predominantly oolitic limestone belt, of which the Cotswolds form the best-known section, stretches from the Dorset coast in the south to Lincolnshire in the East by the North Sea. The limestone rocks of the Cotswolds were formed in shallow tropical seas during the Jurassic Period so named because limestone strata from the period were first identified in the Jura Mountains.

Essentially, the Cotswolds are an exposed section of the outcrop. The major western scarp exposes limestones from the 'Lower' to 'Middle Jurassic' era (roughly between 201.3 and 174.1 million years ago); the classic oolitic 'Cotswold stone' was formed in the 'Middle Jurassic' - from about 174.1 to 163.5 million years ago. The stone is named 'oolitic' because it's made up of small round grains called 'ooiliths' that are stuck together by lime mud. These form in shallow, warm waters where calcium carbonate is deposited from sea water due to evaporation, the round grains growing in size as they are gently rolled to and fro by waves The Cleeve Common Trust describes the process like this: 'As time passed, the sea bed turned to layers of sedimentary rock, which have since been forced upward by geological movement to form the Cotswold Hills'.

Oolitic limestone close up

Source: The Geological Society

Not surprisingly, the Cotswolds are currently home to some fifty national Special Sites of Scientific Interest (SSSIs) on account of their geology. In addition, there are 186 recognised local sites of interest, highlighting the importance of this area for its international educational value to understanding of geology and its specialist sub disciplines, i.e. the study of rock layers and layering (stratigraphy), landforms and the processes shaping them (geomorphology), and ancient life forms (palaeontology).

Great variety - a mix of uplands and lowlands

As well as helping to explain the second part of the name, a landform of a steep scarp crowned by a high open wold, along with a long and rolling dip slope cut by a series of increasingly wooded valleys, makes for a great variety of views. The Cotswold scarp, to paraphrase the NCA profile, provides far reaching expansive views westwards over the Severn Estuary and Avon Vales to Wales, the Malvern Hills and Shropshire Hills, and eastward across and into the Cotswolds. It also provides a dramatic backdrop to Bath, Stroud and Cheltenham. The high wolds, although not as elevated as the scarp, provide extensive uncluttered easterly views across the Vale of White Horse to the North Wessex Downs. Not to be forgotten is that much of the scarp affords panoramic views across adjacent lowlands, framing views outwards and across the Cotswolds landscape itself, with glimpsed views through wooded valleys.

A mix of uplands and lowlands doesn't just influence the views. The NCA profile goes on to draw attention to other key implications:

- Arable farming dominates the high wold and dip slope, while permanent pasture prevails on the steep slopes of the scarp and river valleys, along with pockets of internationally important limestone grassland.
- Drystone walls define the pattern of fields of the high wold and dip slope. Hedgerows form the main field boundaries on the deeper soils and river valleys.
- Ancient beech hangers line stretches of the upper slopes of the scarp, while oak and ash are characteristic of the river valleys. Regular blocks of coniferous and mixed plantations are scattered across the open high wold and dip slope.

• Large areas of common land, important for unimproved calcareous grassland, are characteristic of the scarp and high wold areas.

Overall, says the NCA profile, steep-sided valleys dissect the rolling dip slope characterised by small hedgerow enclosed fields with tree-lined rivers and wet meadows, and parklands. The lush, wetter, more vegetated landscape in the valleys contrasts with the drier exposed high wold. Noticeable, too, is that in the south of the area hedgerows are principally made up of hazel. Elsewhere, most hedgerows were originally planted with hawthorn, helping to account for the different styles of hedge laying traditional to the area.

As a later section emphasises, the mix of terrains is also fundamentally important for both the settlement pattern and economic development of the Cotswolds. Scattered hamlets and isolated farmsteads are found on the higher ground, along with burial sites and hill forts. Smaller towns and villages nestle at the scarp foot, in the valley bottoms and on the gentler valley sides at springlines. The relative prosperity of the Cotswolds similarly owes a great deal to the combination of arable and pasture, the sheep farming on the pasture being especially important in medieval times.

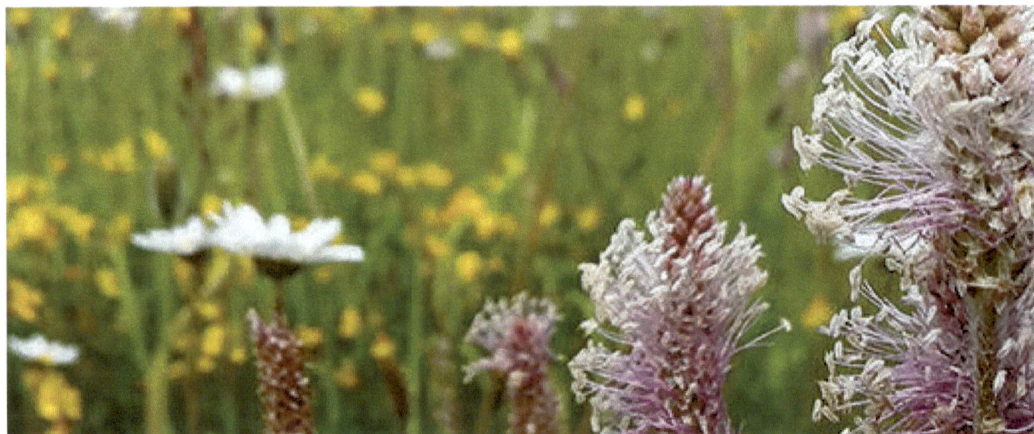

Glorious grasslands

As Cotswold National Landscape emphasises, one of the many benefits stemming from the Cotswolds' bedrock of Jurassic limestone is a type of wildflower-rich grassland habitat rare in the UK. Rodborough Common Special Area of Conservation (SAC) near Stroud, for example, is the most extensive area of calcicole grassland, which is more or less confined to the Cotswolds. Although much reduced in recent times, the many scattered remnants of unimproved limestone grassland form a patchwork which makes for a colourful component of the Cotswold landscape throughout spring and summer. Indeed, a typical patch can contain over one hundred species of plants, including national rarities such as pasque flower and Cotswold pennycress. Wildflowers, in turn, support a huge variety of invertebrates, including the Chalkhill Blue, Adonis blue and large blue, and Duke of Burgundy butterflies, particularly on the scarp and high wold.

These invertebrates repay the favour in supporting a variety of mammals, bats, bees and birds higher up the food chain. Thus, farmland birds have a strong association with the high wold due to the mix of arable and pastoral farming activity. Species such as grey partridge, lapwing, turtle dove, tree sparrow and corn bunting have suffered significant declines in population since the 1970s, but their populations remain a key feature. There is also a Bats Special Area of Conservation near Bath embracing Box Mine, Winsley Mines, Combe Down and Bathampton Down Mines, and Brown's Folly.

A variety of woodland

Woodland cover in the Cotswolds, according to Cotswold National Landscape, is estimated to be 20,657 ha or around 10 percent of the AONB area. It mainly comprises broadleaved woodland (65 percent), followed by coniferous woodland (15 percent) and mixed woodland (13 per cent). 'Other' includes felled woodland (245ha), shrub (257 ha) and young trees (842 ha). Ash and beech are the predominant broadleaved species, with approximately 4,400 ha of ash and 4,000 ha of beech. At the western edge of the Cotswolds, oak and mixed broadleaves account for a further 3,000ha. It's the dense beech woods and tree clumps that contribute to an imposing skyline.

The area of woodland in the AONB on ancient woodland sites, the CNL goes on, is 9,292 ha or about 45 percent of woodland cover. Included are 'Ancient & Semi-Natural Woodland' (5,940ha) and 'Plantations on Ancient Woodland Sites' (3,352ha).

Ancient beech woods are a particularly distinct and prominent feature of the Cotswolds – especially along the scarp and incised valleys. Some of this wood is included within a 'Cotswold Beechwoods Special Area of Conservation'. By contrast, mixed oak, ash, sycamore and maple tend to be concentrated on the dip slope, with mixed oak woodlands featuring on the upper slopes of valleys as well as the flat high wold tops. Also, not to be forgotten, are the areas of lowland wood pasture and parkland of the larger estates.

Woodlands can contain a wide and notable range of calcicole shrubs and ground flora. Important habitats include wet meadows, springline flushes (i.e where the water spreads diffusely) and tree lined watercourses along the valley bottoms with alder and willow. Where the landform is characterised by deep valleys around Bath, Stroud and Winchcombe, often accentuated by densely-wooded ridge crests, these woods support species such as Duke of Burgundy butterfly, are floristically rich and important for molluscs. The network also helps to support the Bath and Bradford-on-Avon 'Special Area of Conservation', which is home to 15 percent of the UK's greater horseshoe bat population, alongside Bechstein's bat and lesser horseshoe bat.

Distinctive settlement pattern - small towns and villages

The Cotswolds has a rich settlement history, the NCA profile reminds us, with nationally and internationally important evidence of prehistoric, Roman, medieval and later periods in the form of archaeological sites, historic buildings and the wider landscape. As well as two World Heritage Sites (Bath and Blenheim Palace), the Cotswolds are home to no fewer than 538 'Scheduled Ancient Monuments', a wealth of 'Listed Buildings', 88 registered 'Historic Parks and Gardens' covering 9,177 hectares, two registered battlefields, along with undiscovered buried archaeological assets.

Neolithic barrows and Iron-age hill forts. Two things you won't be able to escape on the Cotswold Way itself are barrows and hill forts dating from the 'Neolithic' *(Stone-age)* and Iron-age respectively. As Tim Copeland puts it in his *Archaeological walking guides: the Cotswold Way* (p. 12,) long barrows are a 'haunting feature' of the Cotswold Way', with at least twenty on it or close by. As for hill forts, he adds (p. 19), they 'dominate the highest and most spectacular hills along the Cotswold Way' - there are as many as sixteen possibilities. The two explainers below spell out some of the technical terms involved to help you better appreciate the descriptions in the stage chapters.

Roman roads and 'villas'. The Romans also left their mark, with their roads criss-crossing the countryside (notably *Akeman Street, Ermine Street and the Fosse Way*). As well as major settlements, such as Bath (*Aquae Sulis*), Cirencester (*Corinium Dobunnorum*) and Gloucester (*Glevum*), the Cotswolds are also reckoned to have had one of the highest concentrations of Roman 'villas' (*Villa rustica or 'rural manors'*) in Britain. Overall, the number is reckoned to be as many as fifty. You'll be meeting one in Chapter 9 - it's Great Witcombe, along with Chedworth north of Cirencester, one of the best examples.

Manors, markets and towns. The Cotswolds are said to be characterised by a 'nucleated' as opposed to a 'dispersed' or 'linear' pattern of settlement. Small towns and villages, in other words, predominate. Such a pattern mainly emerged between the 10th and 12th centuries and is largely the result of a development known as 'manorialism'. Sometimes included in the definition of feudalism, 'manorialism' grew as the result of the crown's increasing centralisation of power and because it was convenient for organising the estates of the aristocracy and church institutions. Its defining features included a large, sometimes fortified, manor house in which the lord of the manor and his dependents administered a rural estate, and a population of labourers or serfs who worked the surrounding land to support themselves and their lord. Initially, these labourers fulfilled their obligations with labour time or in-kind produce; later, as commercial activity increased, cash payment became the norm.

For several centuries before their dissolution in the 1530s, church institutions played an especially important role in 'manorialism'. This is above all true of the north Cotswolds, where the abbeys of Evesham, Hailes, Pershore and Winchcombe were major landowners, along with the Bishopric of Worcester. Effectively, these church lands might be said to have been the 'superstar' companies of their day, making the most of the mixed landscape with low-lying fertile areas for crops and upland areas for livestock. Notable, too, was the extent of their ownership reach. The Bishop of Worcester, for example, held the manor of Blockley, which was some twenty five miles away from his base; he is also reported as having 1,000 sheep on Cleeve Common in 1246 - which is about twenty miles or 32 kms from Blockley in almost the opposite direction!

As for the emergence of towns, Tim Copeland reminds us in his guide cited earlier (p. 21) that the exploitation of commerce, trade and revenues was the main motivation. A key instrument was the granting of a royal charter to establish a market. Another was the promotion of villages to borough status, which brought with it the right of landowners to 'burgage', i.e. require rent in return for tenure.

In both cases, there was an impact on the physical shape of the settlement. Thus, markets helped to structure town layout - market areas with their Woolstaplers' Halls were

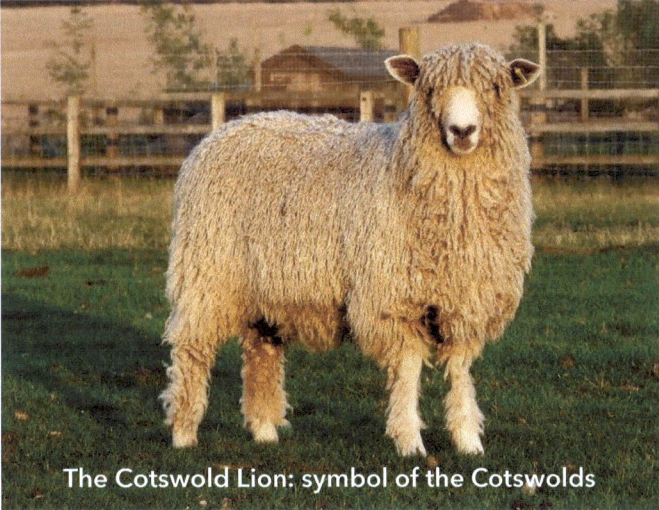

The Cotswold Lion: symbol of the Cotswolds

Source: Cotswold Family Holidays

usually triangular or square. Similarly, the right to 'burgage' freehold tenure for rent typically led to a continuous row of houses alongside the main road with a narrow street frontage and a longish back plot. Which is why you will find streets in some towns called 'Back Lanes' or 'Back Ends' to this day.

In the Cotswolds, several well known market towns developed during the 12th and 13th centuries on the back of the wealth generated by the wool trade - examples on the trail include Wotton-under-Edge, Painswick and Chipping Campden. As well as houses and schools, the most striking as well as long lasting legacy to the landscape from the wool merchants' fortunes are the Cotswolds' famous 'wool churches'. As well as Chipping Campden on the trail, examples are to be found in Burford, Chipping Norton, Cirencester, Fairford and Northleach.

In a second phase, there was a move to cloth making. The presence of the water to drive the wheels of the mills was critical here, helping to explain why balance of advantage shifted south to areas around Wotton, Dursley, Painswich and, above all, the Stroud Valley. The legacy here are the mill buildings and their owners' houses.

The Cotswold Lion: an essential ingredient. The breed of sheep on which the wealth of the emerging Cotswold towns was based is known as the *Cotswold Lion*. They have a long history and, most probably, were bred from the long wool sheep introduced by the Romans for whom they were also a very important part of the economy. As Copeland reminds us, the 'Seasons' mosaic at Chedworth Villa shows 'Winter' dressed in a *Birrus Britannicus* - a hooded cloak made of wool.

Whatever their origin, absolutely clear is that the *Cotswold Lion* seem to have found the limestone grasslands much to their liking, being nicknamed the 'Golden Fleece' breed. In the words of the 12th century saying, 'In Europe the best wool is English and in England the best wool is Cotswold'. A heavy forelock falling over the face, they remain the symbol of the Cotswolds and the CNL's newsletter carries their name. Today, with the economics meaning meat makes more money than wool, they are no longer to be found on the Cotswolds pastures. You can still see examples, though, if you go to the Cotswold Farm Park where *Countryfile's* Adam Henson keeps rare breeds.

Vernacular architecture - local limestone brings harmony

One of the things that strikes people coming to the Cotswolds for the first time is the similarity of the architecture - it's almost as if just one person or group of people designed the lot. A major consideration in the development of the vernacular architecture is the limestone that has featured so much in the chapter. Quarries abound across the Cotswolds, albeit most are no longer worked. According to the Geological Society, limestone is used for building because it easily splits into blocks and is quite weather-resistant. Very clear is that its colour creates a strong sense of place and unity which carries through to the buildings and walls which have been built using local limestone for centuries. In Bath and the south of the region, the colour' is quite pale; in Chipping Campden and the north, it's more honey coloured. The distinctive character of the area is reflected not just in its wonderful buildings, moreover, but also in its dry stone walls utilising locally quarried stone. There are reckoned to be around 4,000 miles (6,400 kms) of such walls in the Cotswolds. Stone masons supposedly say that true 'Cotsallers' can do anything with stone except eat it!

Tranquillity and calm

The Cotswolds have come to be seen as something of a country idyll with a timeless quality, helping to explain the large estates scattered across the area, such as Blenheim Palace, Sherborne Park, Dyrham Park and Dodington Park. Their presence isn't perhaps surprising. A largely rural area with a distinctive settlement pattern of small towns and villages, with principal cities lying at its edges, means levels of intrusion are low away from settlements and main transport routes. There is also little disturbance from noise or light pollution. Low dry stone walls are prominent on the high wold, enclosing large arable fields and adding to a sense of openness and harmony across the area. In the Victorian era especially, the Cotswolds also came to be somewhat idealised for their lack of industrialisation and development as well as their vernacular architecture and archaeological features.

As later chapters will explain in more detail, places like Broadway and Chipping Campden became a magnet for composers such as Elgar and Vaughan Williams, artists (for example, John Singer, Davis 'Frank' Millet and Edwin Austin Abbey), and writers such as J. M. Barrie, along with key figures in the arts and crafts movement more generally - William Morris and C.R. Ashbee are good examples. The furniture designer Gordon Russell grew up in Broadway and had a workshop in the town. More recently, the patronage of members of the Royal family and a number of celebrities has helped to add to the lustre - Prince Charles has his country residence at Highgrove near Tetbury and Princess Anne hers at Gatcombe park near Minchinhampton. Sir James Dyson owns Dodington Park.

The practical benefit of this feature of the Cotswolds is that it has attracted individual benefactors who have made a very considerable difference either in terms of making improvements or preventing damaging development. As later chapters will again explain in more detail, examples include the artist and etcher Frederick Landseer Griggs, who ensured that Dover's Hill came into National Trust hands and Sir Philp Stott, the famous mill designer, who helped to rescue a run-down Stanton and make it what it is today.

Footpaths in abundance

Such is the landscape and settlement pattern that the Cotswolds are blessed with over 3,000 miles (4,800 kms) of footpaths and bridleways according to Wikipedia. Many go back to Anglo-Saxon times and were originally created by people walking from one settlement to another or to work, the local market, the next village, church and, later, school. Sometimes those associated with the church were designated 'mass paths' and 'corpse roads'.

An example of a corpse road, suggests Wikipedia, involves St Peter and Paul at Blockley, which held the burial right to the inhabitants in the near-by hamlets of Stretton-on-Fosse and Aston Magna. Both had chapels, but 'tithes' and 'mortuaries' were owed to the Blockley church, to which the people were committed to carry their deceased for burial. The corpse road from Aston to Blockley churchyard was over two miles (3 kms) long and crossed three small streams en route. The one from Stretton ran for some four miles (6 kms) and crossed two streams.

There were also footpaths created by those undertaking a pilgrimage. Just to quote one example, the British Pilgrimage Trust tells us that William of Malmesbury, writing in the twelfth century, reported that 'there was no place in England to which more pilgrims travelled than to Winchcombe on Kenelm's feast day'. This is because Winchcombe was where Kenelm's body was eventually buried after he'd been murdered by his sister's lover in the Clent Hills, near Birmingham, in AD 819 or thereabouts before he could become King of Mercia.

St Kenelm's Well with stone and tree guardians

Source: The British Pilgrimage Trust

You'll find further details of a host of self guided walks if you go to the *Cotswold Gateway* maps on the Cotswold National Landscape website. Similarly, many of the towns and villages on the Cotswold Way route publish details of local walks in their vicinity. Perhaps most notable are Dursley, Wotton-under-Edge and Winchcombe, which are Walkers are Welcome towns with annual walking festivals. The Cotswolds are also home to several other long distance trails, making it easy for you to explore the entire area. These include:

- *Wychavon Way* - (42 miles) from Droitwich to Broadway
- *Winchcombe Way* – (42 miles) a figure-of-eight trail centred on Winchcombe
- *Wardens Way* - (14 miles) and Windrush Way (14 miles) links Winchcombe with Bourton-on-the-Water
- *Monarchs Way* - (615 miles) passes through the Cotswolds
- *Macmillan Way* - (290 miles) passes through the Cotswolds

Explainer: Know your barrows

To paraphrase Historic England, the barrows you'll come across in the Cotswolds are of two main types: long barrows and round barrows.

Long barrows date from as early as 3800 BCE. Externally, they comprise a large mound rarely more than about 50 metres in length and up to 25 metres in width. Sometimes they are slightly oval in form, often with one end wider and higher than the other. Invariably there are ditches alongside from where the construction material may have come. Additions to the length and height effectively make some mounds much larger and monumental in nature with some excessively long mounds appearing to be the product of two end-to-end long barrows.

Round barrows date to around 3000 BCE. Size varies from examples of only 5 or 6 m across to those that take on monumental proportions of over 50 m diameter and 6 m in height. Most common, because of their shape, is the bowl barrow with slopes of varying profile, sometimes with a surrounding ditch and occasionally an outer bank.

The underlying structures of barrow mounds can comprise stone platforms, pits, stone cairns or turf mounds, various timber structures, wooden and stone chambers, circles, pits and post holes. They can also conceal ceremonial structures such as henges.

Deposits of pottery and stone tools are not unusual, along with animal and human bones. Sometimes these indicate formal burials, with an entire skeleton present, placed in a grave beneath or near the mound.

According to the Wikipedia entry, long barrows originated in the area of modern Spain, Portugal and western France. It then spread along the Atlantic coast, reflecting sea trade routes of the times. Their purpose and meaning, though, remains a puzzle. One view is that they were religious sites - perhaps part of a system of ancestor veneration. Or they could have had economic significance - territorial markers of the areas controlled by communities as they transitioned toward farming.

- *Heart of England Way* - (101 miles) from Staffordshire to Bourton on the Water
- *Gloucestershire Way* - (94 miles) From Chepstow to Tewkesbury.
- *Diamond Way* - (65 miles) from Northleach in the south to near Chipping Campden in the north, Guiting Power in the west to near Bourton on the Water in the east
- *Wysis Way* - (55 miles) from Monmouth to Kemble to link Offa's Dyke, the Cotswold Way and Thames Path National Trails.

As a matter of interest, you might also like to know that, under its constitution, the CWA also supports a number of 'other named trails' initially meaning those trails that cross the Cotswolds (Heart of England Way, Macmillan Way and Monarch's Way) and locally based Cotswold trails (Diamond Way, Gloucestershire Way, Wardens' Way, Windrush Way, Winchcombe Way and Wychavon Way). This list was agreed at the first AGM and published on the CWA website. It is subject to review and/or confirmation each year.

Explainer: Know your hill forts

Hill forts are amongst the most striking of all archaeological monuments, says Historic England, their locations and often massive earthworks making a very powerful statement about the organisation, skills, and beliefs of Iron Age peoples. As the name implies, hill forts are defended places surrounded by one or more circuits of banks and ditches and generally placed on hilltops, ridges, spurs or promontories.

The first hill forts were probably built shortly after 900 BCE, with the main building phase beginning later between 800 and 700 BCE. After the end of this period, most hill forts were abandoned, although a few had Roman camps built within them. Later, particularly in the middle of the 4th century AD, many temples were built within hill forts. In the post-Roman period (AD 450-700), several hill forts were re-fortified.

The defensive works of early hill forts usually consist of a bank and an external ditch. They are known as 'univallate' forts. Later, about 400 BCE, these often 'developed' into 'bivallate' and 'multivallate' forms with more bank and ditch added, some involving several circuits. Where hill forts occupy the ends of spurs, they are called 'promontory forts'.

Though seen primarily as defended sites, there is little evidence of warfare at hill forts - the case of Crickley Hill in Chapter 9 is an exception. 'The bulk of the evidence', in Copeland's words (p. 20), suggests that hill forts 'would have been symbolically defensive rather than practically so, and warfare was primarily about being threatening to your enemies rather than entering into open conflict with them'

As with barrows, there is much debate about the purposes of hill forts. They are likely, though, to have included agricultural functions such as storing food and corralling livestock from the farms and fields below. They might also have fulfilled the role of meeting places and, perhaps, religious centres. Complicating matters is that the variation is immense. Some hill forts were flourishing and important places which lasted for some time; others appear never to have been extensively used.

Chapter 3
More than you might have expected
Bath to Cold Ashton

Walking out of big cities is not normally very enjoyable - especially if it means leaving the wonderful sights of a city like Bath. In this case, however, you have an exception to the rule. Those who designed the Cotswold Way have done everything they can to get you into the countryside as quickly as possible. The route also has much more to offer that you might have imagined: a stretch up and across open farmland to get you going, iron age vantage points, the highest flat race course in the country, signs of a Roman presence, a high-tech centre for command training and incident simulation, delightful passages through beechwoods, and two manor houses with their stories to tell. If that's not enough, you have a famous battle site from the first English civil war and poignant reminders of what it meant to some of the key participants.

Off to the races

From the start of the Cotswold Way at Bath Abbey, the trail gives you the chance to see the architectural delights of the Circus and Royal Crescent before heading out to open country. Thereafter, it's more or less uphill, with fine views, to Kelston and Bath race course.

As you walk along the side of Primrose's Hill, and after Weston, look out on the right for sight of Beckford Tower rising up on the far hill above the treetops. Built between 1826 and 1827, and originally known as Lansdown Tower, the structure is essentially a folly. In the words of the Wikipedia entry, 'The tower was built for William Thomas Beckford, a rich novelist, art collector and critic, to designs by Henry Goodridge, and was completed in 1827'. Beckford used it as a library and a retreat, with the cupola at the top acting as a belvedere providing views over the surrounding countryside. The Italianate building at the base of the tower housed drawing rooms and a library. Extensive grounds between Beckford's house in Lansdown Crescent and the tower were landscaped and planted to create 'Beckford's Ride'. The building, says the Bath Preservation Trust which owns and operates Beckford's Tower and its Museum, was once home to one of the greatest collections of books, furniture and art in Georgian England'. It now stands as the only surviving example of William Beckford's great architectural achievements.

The Trust explains that Beckford's ability to build, and to collect, was made possible by the wealth he inherited and accumulated as a slavery owner of Jamaican sugar plantations. He also received compensation from the government following the abolition of slavery.

Bath Abbey - the start of the Cotswold Way

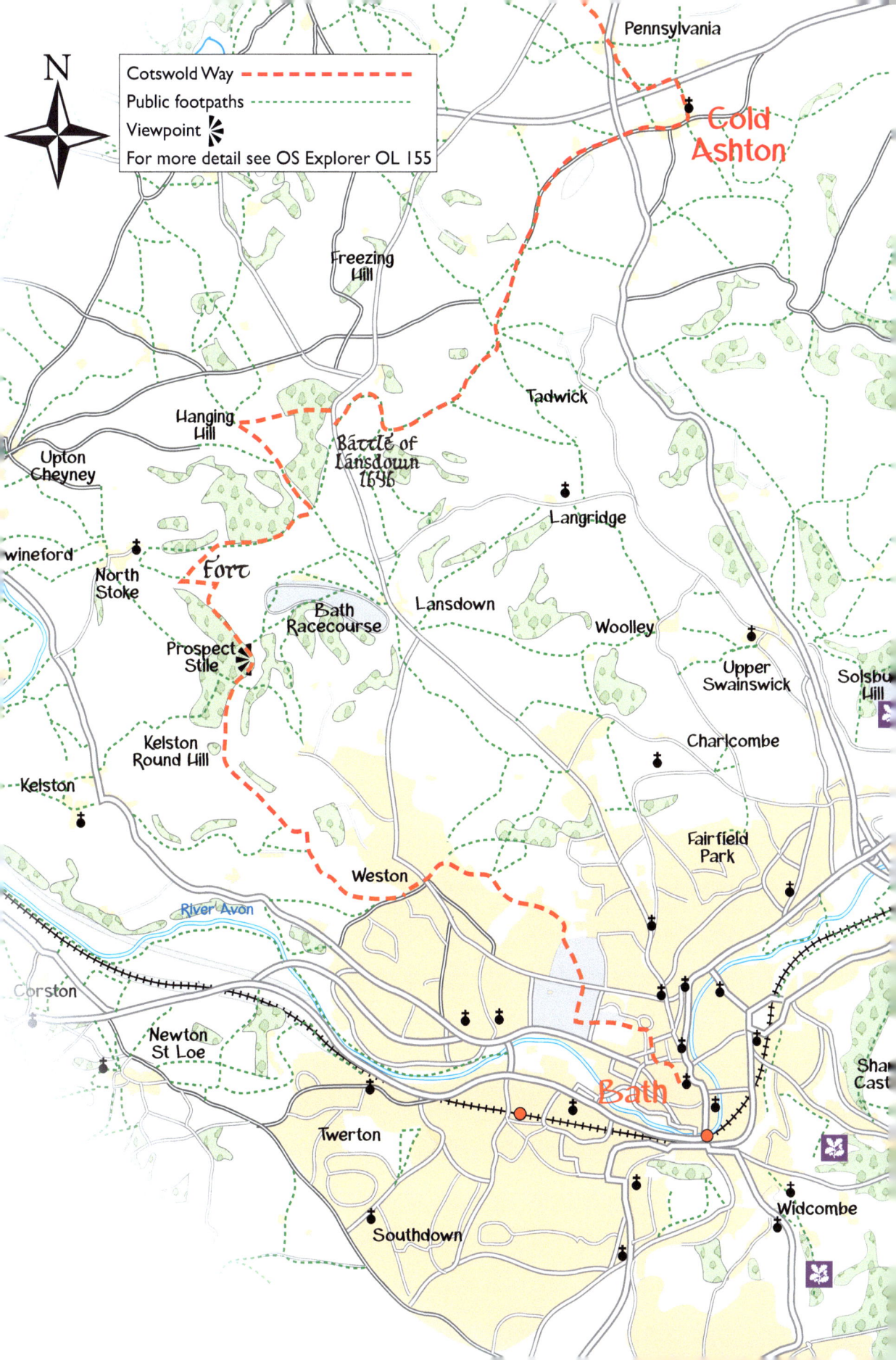

N

For more detail see OS Explorer OL 155

Legend:
- Cotswold Way
- Public footpaths
- Viewpoint

Pennsylvania

Cold Ashton

Freezing Hill

Tadwick

Hanging Hill

Battle of Lansdown 1646

Upton Cheyney

Langridge

wineford

North Stoke

Fort

Lansdown

Woolley

Bath Racecourse

Prospect Stile

Upper Swainswick

Solsbu Hill

Kelston Round Hill

Charlcombe

Kelston

Fairfield Park

Weston

River Avon

Corston

Newton St Loe

Bath

Sha Cast

Twerton

Widcombe

Southdown

Beckford previously had built a massive gothic revival house in Wilshire called Fonthill Abbey ('Beckford's Folly') whose spire collapsed soon after it was completed. Beckford had, wisely as it turned out, already sold it by then.

Weston itself was originally a separate village, becoming a suburb of Bath, as the city grew. The earliest evidence of occupation comes from two Celtic caddy spoons found in the village in 1825. These are believed to have been used as ceremonial anointing regalia.

During the 10th century, Weston was divided into two estates. One, on the slopes of Lansdown, was given by Edmund I to Aethelare in 946. Two manors with 41 households are recorded in the Domesday Book of 1086: one held by Bath Abbey and the other by Arnulf de Hesding. They continued to be leased to tenants until the dissolution of the monasteries in the late 1530s, after which they reverted to ownership of the king.

Weston was also the birthplace of Saint Alphege. Born around 954, Alphege Ælfheah, had been an anchorite (i.e. a recluse) before being elected abbot of Bath Abbey. His reputation for piety and sanctity led to his promotion to the episcopate and, eventually, to his becoming Archbishop of Canterbury, furthering the cult of Dunstan and encouraging learning. He was canonised in 1078 after being captured by Viking raiders during the siege of Canterbury in 1011 and killed by them after refusing to allow himself to be ransomed. .

You'll pass Weston All Saints church, where worship has been carried out for 800 years. The present church, though, was only built in 1832, its 15th century predecessor proving not large enough. If you search the graveyard, you might find the grave of Mr Oliver of 'Bath Oliver Biscuit' fame.

On route after Weston are two famous vantage points giving you wide ranging views across the countryside. The first of these is Kelston Roundhill, which is an ancient barrow - it's believed that Kelston translates as 'Hill of the Celts'. Close to the small, rural village lying between Bath and Bristol, it's well-known amongst local walkers thanks to the intersection of several public footpaths at its heart. The most popular walk here is the 'Kelston Roundhill Walk' - which incorporates part of the Cotswold Way - offering breathtaking views from the top. On a clear day you'll be able to see both Severn bridges, across to Wales and the Black Mountains, the Wiltshire Downs to the East and the Mendip Hills to the South.

Prospect Stile, which follows fairly quickly, is where the Cotswold Voluntary Wardens have done a lot of clearing work and installed a welcome seat. Here again you have wonderful views across the Avon Valley to the Mendips and a topograph to help identify all the features. It's well worth the walk to get here: you get a close up view of Kelston Roundhill and in the distance to the west, the Black Mountains in Wales.

As the Bathscape Partnership explains, there are great walking routes to get here, as well as the Cotswold Way national trail. Your walk can start in the city centre, at *Newbridge Park & Ride* or from the village of Kelston, which has local amenities, or a shorter level walk from the *Lansdown Park & Ride*.

The trail now skirts around Bath racecourse. The Wikipedia entry tells us that it's a left-handed oval track of one mile four furlongs and 25 yards, with a run-in of nearly half-a-mile. The home straight is 4 furlongs, with a steady rise and turn. At 780 feet (238 metres) above sea level, it's the highest flat racecourse in the country and has no watering facility, so the going can become very firm during a dry summer. Only the National Hunt courses at Hexham and Exeter are higher. Racing was first recorded at Bath in 1728. In 1811, the first major meet at Bath Racecourse was held, under the auspices of a local family, the Blathwayts who will feature again in Chapter 4. Originally there was just one meet

Prospect Style toposcope

a year at the course, lasting for two days, but gradually over the years, the number increased to its present level of twenty-two. In the early years, the Somerset Stakes was the major race of the calendar, and this race is still held annually. There were a number of grandstand buildings in those days and people used to watch the races from their carriages lined up beside the track.

You might like to know that, during World War II, the racecourse was used as a landing field by the Royal Air Force and named RAF North Stoke. In 1953, it was also the site of a criminal plot surrounding the 'Spa selling plate'. Having two horses that looked almost identical, the gang substituted a good horse for a poor one. They bet heavily on the substituted horse and damaged the power supply to the racecourse preventing the bookmakers from changing the odds, which remained at 10-1. The horse won the race and the gang would have profited highly had not racing officials become suspicious and called in Scotland Yard. The gang were subsequently brought to justice.

The Romans were here

Following the Cotswold Way to the north will take you to a fantastic viewpoint on a tight corner of this most southerly of Cotswold Hills escarpments. It has the best of views north, west and south as it juts out from the most westerly point of the entire scarp line extending from Hanging Hill to the north-east and Dean Hill in the south-east. It's the site of *Little Down Fort* and Roman camp. *Little Down Fort*, sometimes known as 'North Stoke Promontory Fort' in recognition of the small village of the same name nearby, is the first of many that you pass on the trail. Historic England describes the fort like this:

The monument includes a large univallate hillfort containing a bowl barrow and pillow mounds, situated on the summit of a prominent projecting spur of Lansdown Hill known as Little Down, overlooking the valley of the River Avon. The hillfort survives as a triangular enclosure defined by a scarp on two sides above steep natural slopes and by a stone-faced rampart bank of up to 2m high with an outer ditch of up to 3m deep on the eastern side. The entrance is to the east and historically further outworks were recorded, including counterscarp banks and a defended entrance to the north. These are no longer clearly identifiable on the ground as surface remains but elements of them will survive as buried features. Within the interior are two low rectangular mounds which were excavated in 1911 in the belief that they were barrows. Excavation demonstrated that they were in fact pillow mounds. A further, crescent-shaped bank of up to 0.5m high is interpreted as a bowl barrow.

You may remember meeting 'bowl barrows' in the previous chapter - they are a type of burial mound or tumulus used to cover a tomb and get their name, not surprisingly, from resemblance to an upturned bowl. In case you're wondering, 'pillow mounds' are artificial warrens built to house rabbits to be farmed for their fur and meat. Long and low earthworks, they are usually cigar-shaped and in groups. The 'Right of Free Warren' required a licence and people who looked after pillow mounds were called warreners.

Pipley Wood, which you come to next, is classed as ancient woodland; it has been forested since at least 1600 and the time of the first Ordnance Survey map. Walking through the wood, you can still see old field boundary banks and ditches, some with ancient trees from old hedgerows. There is very little written history, though; references to the parish simply say that the area is 'mostly grazing'. There is, nevertheless, a great deal of history in the area. There are Roman remains very close to the wood, including those of a fort to the south west and a villa to the east.

Also, Pipley Wood is home to many plants and animals. Its canopy is made up of ash, sycamore and hazel trees with the occasional mature oak. Smaller plants include dog's mercury, bluebells, tufted hair-grass and dogtails, with mosses and ferns much in evidence. A visual record of the plants and animals in Pipley Wood exists thanks to one of its Artists in Residence drawing many examples of the flora and fauna to be found there.

Animals too can be found in abundance in the woods with foxes, roe deer, grey squirrels, rabbits, wood mice, bank voles and badgers all present. There is even evidence of dormice nesting in the woods.

Flitting from tree to tree are many bird species including resident breeders such as woodpeckers (green and great spotted), buzzards, sparrowhawks, owls (tawny and little), wagtails and wrens, as well as declining species such as song thrushes and bullfinches. Insects such as dragonflies, grasshoppers, crickets, hover flies and butterflies abound. In fact, over 27 species of butterfly have been recorded in Pipley Wood, three of them very rare ('Wood White', 'Pearl Bordered Fritillary' and the 'Silver-washed Fritillary').

Just beyond Pipley Wood is Pipley Barn, the country home of Henry Lawrence (more properly, Sir Henry Lawrence, a hereditary Baronet) lying in the centre of a 55 acre estate of woodland, pasture. Nearby the 'Grim Reaper' and other mysterious steel statues cause you to pause in reflection.

Just below the edge of the golf course is a Roman settlement (possibly a villa) and prehistoric or Roman enclosures (possibly a field system) at Brockham End. Fragments of dry walls, a well, three stone coffins containing skeletons, an altar, occultist's stamp and pottery sherds dating from the 1st to 4th century have been found, along with Iron Age coin and pottery.

Fragments of dry walls at different angles, many burnt stones and a well, 4 ft. in diameter and 17-18 ft. deep, were dug out by Sir Alexander Lawrence 100 yards north of his house, Brockham End, North Stoke. Three R.B. type coffins of local oolite, containing skeletons, were found, one also containing [sandal] nails. Other finds included a Roman altar, an occultist's stamp and R.B. pottery sherds. Excavations at Brockham End in 1939 and 1946-8 produced pottery ranging from Flavian to 4th c. A.D. and two sherds of Iron Age 'A'. A debased silver coin of the Dobunii (first half of 1st c. A.D.) was also found. A stone coffin against a wall at ST 7157 6974 coincides with the O.S. siting symbol. Excavation trenches survive at ST 7160 6972 but nothing can be interpreted from them.

Just after Hanging Hill is the South West Command Development Centre (SWCDC) for Avon Fire & Rescue. It's a high-tech centre for command training and incident simulation, says the website, using a full range of tools, including 'XVR' and 'Hydra'. 'XVR' scenarios, apparently, are designed 'to provide incident commanders with a safe training environment as close to a real incident as possible, focusing on local risks and tailor made training scenarios to challenge incident commanders'. The

The Grim Reaper near Pipley

'Hydra' tool allows 'a dedicated learning experience focusing on decision making and exploring reasons why those decisions were made at the time'.

As well as having an impressive portfolio of current activities, the site has an interesting past. It was commissioned at the time of the 'cold war' of the late 1940s/early 1950s, and completed in 1954, to counter the A-bomb threat delivered by enemy aircraft. Named as the 'Anti-Aircraft Operations Room' for 'Gun Defended Area Bristol Group 2', it was primarily involved with the defence of Bristol with its industrial and port sites considered as prime targets.

The Battle of Lansdown

The section of the trail between Hanging Hill and Freezing Hill Lane is also the site of one of the major engagements in the first English Civil War of 1642 to 1646 - the Battle of Lansdown. Altogether you'll find four interpretation panels erected by the local authorities (it is right on the border of South Gloucestershire and Bath & NE Somerset), to help you put everything into context: one on the summit at the west end of Hanging Hill, two beside the road near the Grenville monument and one at the eastern edge of the scarp. Other signs include a series of ten metal orange coloured 'standards' on blue poles that mark the trail along the edge of the scarp.

Especially prominent is the monument to Sir Bevil Grenville, which is under the care of English Heritage. It was erected in 1720 by Lord Lansdown, Sir Bevil's grandson, and said to be one of the oldest surviving war memorials. Sir Bevil was a royalist commander during the first English Civil War and the monument commemorates his heroism in the Battle of Lansdowne, where he died in hand-to-hand fighting leading his Cornish pikemen.

As for the battle itself, the story goes that, by late May 1643, Lord Hopton's royalist army had captured most of the south west of England and was advancing eastwards. Sir William Waller's Parliamentarian army held Bath and sought to obstruct Hopton's further advance. On 2 July 1643 the Royalists seized the bridge at Bradford on Avon. On 3 July, skirmishes took place at Claverton and at Waller's positions south and east of Bath. Waller thereupon occupied a strong position on Lansdown Hill, northwest of Bath, while the main Royalist force moved north through Batheaston to Marshfield.

According to The Battlefield Trust, the key facts are that, after several probing moves to the south and east of the city, the armies finally engaged on 5th July, the battle starting in the morning and lasting all day. The Royalists numbered about 4000 foot, 2000 horse and 300 dragoons; the Parliamentarians about 1500 foot and 2500 horse.

The interpretation panels along the ridge describe the evolution of the battle. The Battlefield Trust also gives us a strong flavour of the cut and thrust as attack and counterattack ensued throughout the day:

> Waller had taken a commanding position on Lansdown Hill. He sent troops forward to skirmish with the royalist cavalry detachments and finally forced the royalists to deploy and then to engage. After initial success on Tog Hill, a mile or more to the north, his forces were eventually forced to retreat. Now Hopton took the initiative and made direct and flanking attacks up the steep slopes of Lansdown Hill. Despite heavy losses amongst the regiments of horse and foot in the centre, under musket and artillery fire, the royalists finally gained a foothold on the scarp edge. Repeated cavalry charges failed to dislodge them and Waller was finally forced to retire, as he was outflanked by attacks through the woods on either side.

> He retreated a few hundred yards to the cover of a wall across the narrowest point of the plateau. As darkness fell the fire-fight continued. Neither army would move from the cover they had found and both armies contemplated retreat. Late that night, under the cover of darkness, it was the parliamentarians who abandoned their position. Though the royalists were left in control of the field and of Bath, they had bought the ground at a high cost. Waller in contrast had lost very few killed or wounded and was ready to fight another day.

In what might be said to have been an inconclusive battle, the Royalists suffered possibly 200-300 killed and many wounded. The Parliamentarians escaped with just 20 killed and less than 60 wounded.

Adding to the Royalists' misfortune, an ammunition cart exploded the day after the battle. Hopton was injured and temporarily blinded. The loss of the powder and the absence of most of their horses meant the Royalists could not fight another action. Hopton's army retreated in low spirits to Devizes. Meanwhile, Waller retired to Bath where he awaited reinforcements.

Making the Battle of Lansdown especially poignant is that the two main protagonists, Waller and Hopton, had apparently been close friends before the war. Waller is remembered for a letter he wrote in 1643 to Hopton:

> That great God who is the searcher of my heart knows with what a sad sense I go upon this service, and with what a perfect hatred I detest this war without an enemy;... We are both upon the stage and must act such parts as are assigned us in this tragedy, let us do it in a way of honour, and without personal animosities.

Apparently, too, Hopton's army was in such a poor situation before their retreat that Waller offered him hospitality in Bath, though it was refused. As for Grenville, according to the 1911 *Encyclopædia Britannica*, 'His death was a blow from which the king's cause in the West never recovered, for he alone knew how to handle the Cornishmen. Hopton they revered and respected, but Grenville they loved as peculiarly their own commander …'

You might like to know that, after the inconclusive Battle of Lansdown on 5 July, there was a round two just a couple of weeks later near Devizes. Hopton was joined by Royalist reinforcements and on 13 July, the combined force destroyed Waller's army at Roundway Down, including many from the Bristol garrison. Waller and around 500 cavalry managed to escape to Bristol, but not wishing to be trapped in the city depleted of many of his forces, he and his remaining troops made their way to Evesham on 21 July. Four days later, Bristol surrendered to Prince Rupert, leaving Parliamentarian forces in the west confined to isolated garrisons in Plymouth and elsewhere. Roundway Down was reckoned to be the biggest Royalist success of the war.

Onwards to Cold Ashton

After the battlefield, the trail takes you down into the delightful Hamswell and Swainswick Valley, described by *Country Walking magazine* as one of the undiscovered gems of the Cotswolds. The trail then crosses a ford and then up to Cold Ashton via Greenway Lane. On the left is the Hamswell estate and Hamswell House. Hamswell was one of the three manor houses in the parish of Cold Ashton granted to the Priors of Bath in AD 921 by Athelstan, Alfred the Great's grandson and first king of all England. The Priors owned it until the dissolution of the monasteries in the late 1530s when it was sold to Sir Walter Denys.

A few years later, in 1543, Robert Whittington took a lease on the manor house. Yes, you've probably guessed, he was a descendant of the famous Dick Whittington, thrice Lord Mayor of London, who 'turned again' on his trip to the capital. Robert's grandson, William Whittington was able to buy the house and the estate in 1622 and he and his successors owned them for over 300 years. Occupants during the last century included Lord Justice Maugham, the Lord Chancellor and brother of the novelist Somerset Maughan, and Major General Sir Charles Bonham Carter, the Governor of Malta. The house is now lived in by Rupert and Victoria Legge and their family, who let out the grounds for wedding marquees. By strange coincidence, in 1347, Rupert's ancestor Sir Thomas Legge was elected as the first ever Lord Mayor of London. Like Dick Whittington, he was elected Mayor three times, but as far as is known he didn't have a cat.

Cold Ashton is your final destination on this stage. The village gets its name from 'Farmstead by the ash-tree', v. æsc, tūn. 'Cold' (v. cald, Latin 'frigidus') from its situation, 'much exposed to the violence of the winds'. It's mentioned in the Domesday Book and its origins go back much further, being the site of two round barrows known as 'Robin Hood's butts'. Originally the property of Bath Abbey until the dissolution, the Cold Ashton estate came into the hands of William Pepwall, Mayor of Bristol in 1564 .

There are a number of listed buildings within the village, perhaps the most notable being the Manor House. It has been suggested that this house may date from Pepwall's time and so be described as Elizabethan. More likely, however, is that it was begun in c1629 when John Gunning, another Mayor of Bristol, bought the estate.

The forecourt wall has an impressive ornamental gateway bearing the coat of arms of Sir Robert Gunning of 1678. The archway is a fine example of the renaissance style, with square Roman Doric columns, rosette frieze, surmounted by two floricated urns. Semi-circular steps leading onto the road complete the design and there is a mounting block to one side. Inside the Manor, the most notable feature is the splendid hall screen, one of few in the country to survive intact.

Adjacent to the Manor lies the Old Rectory which dates from the 16th century and was largely rebuilt in the 19th century. It's the place where Sir Bevil Grenville, Royalist Leader in the Civil War died, after being mortally wounded in the Battle of Lansdown described above.

Cold Ashton Manor

Cotswold Way Circular Walk

This stage gives us one of the twelve Cotswold Way Circular Walks. It's No 12. and called 'Journey's End' (because the sequencing goes north-south). In the words of the National Trails website:

'Discover a true sense of pilgrimage with this wonderful walk into the heart of Bath and the southern end of the Cotswold Way. Follow the trail as it slides from open hilltop into historic city, winding its way around open farmland and down bustling alleyways to its crescendo at the majestic splendour of Bath Abbey.'

- Distance: 6 miles (linear – public transport return). Duration: 3½ -4 hours (plus max. ½ hr return)
- Difficulty: Moderate – one stile, some steep sections'.
- You can download the map from www.nationaltrail.co.uk

Battlefield Walks

The Battlefield Trust website gives details of two circular walks for those particularly interested in appreciating how the terrain influenced the passage of the Battle of Landsdown. The Trust adds that the details are meant to be used in conjunction with the downloadable Battlefield OS Explorer map.

Scarp edge walk: 5km (3 ml): an easy walk over fairly level ground on a well marked path with well maintained gates and stiles, providing stunning views across the whole battlefield. In order to avoid the steep descents and ascents involved in the longer circular walk, on this route it is necessary to retrace one's steps from the two extremities of Lansdown Hill.

Circular walk: 7.5 km (4.5ml): a more demanding walk which covers much of the scarp edge walk but also involves two long steep descents and ascents of Freezing Hill and Lansdown Hill and 2km of walking on narrow but very quiet minor roads. To avoid the very dangerous, busy and fast road from Freezing Hill to Tog Hill, which is narrow and lacks any verge, this walk requires a retracing of one's steps to and from Freezing Hill.

NB The Battlefield Trust warns walkers that traffic on the main roads that cross the battlefield is very heavy and fast and so great care must be taken when crossing these roads. Also there are no toilets, pubs or shops anywhere on the battlefield. The nearest toilets will be found at the picnic site car park on Tog Hill, off the A420.

Car Parking

- For the start in Bath, you're best advised to use Landsdown Park and Ride (BA1 9BJ) near the Racecourse.
- Cold Ashton, your destination, has a small car park at the village hall (nearest post code is BS37 4EW).

Chapter 4
Two grand estates
Cold Ashton to Little Sodbury

If you look at the OS map, you might be put off by the sight of the M4 dissecting this stage of the Cotswold Way. Don't worry too much. You'll hear the noise of the M4 motorway as you get close, but it doesn't last for long. There is also a great deal that awaits you on either side of the crossing. You have two grand estates and several churches to see all with interesting tales to tell. You can also visit two more famous hill forts and learn about yet another very important battle - this one taking place in Britain's so-called 'dark ages' and critical in shaping the country's development. Just at the end you can pass the manor house where William Tyndale started the career that led to the first English-language version of the bible.

All things Dyrham

Leaving Cold Ashton, the trail crosses the A46 and brings you very quickly to Pennsylvania. In case you're wondering, this place name didn't cross the Atlantic to become the name of the US state. Rather, it seems, the opposite is true. The name is said to reflect the presence of Quaker families in the village who wanted to recognise the contribution of William Penn to the establishment of that state.

As you head towards the M4, you'll be walking through Dyrham Wood, followed by the estate and the village of the same name - Dyrham, or Deorham as it was, means 'deer enclosure'. Dyrham Wood is where you will find a very special message book shortly after the trail leaves Pennsylvania. First put there in 1995 by a lady from Pennsylvania and now refreshed by the Cotswold Warden who regularly patrols this section of the trail, it allows walkers to record their experiences of walking the Cotswold Way. If you'd like to read some of the fascinating entries and personal stories, you'll find them in the 'Dyrham Wood Message Box' on the Cotswold Way Association website. Don't forget to add your message when you're passing.

The village of Dyrham is very small - along with Hinton close by, the population is less than 300. As in many villages, facilities have declined as personal transport improved. Gone are the school, pub, shop and post office; only the church remains. Otherwise the essential character of the parish remains with several of the small Cotswold stone cottages being Grade II listed. Especially beautiful is the church of St Peter, which dates from 1280, considerably older than the grand mansion next door. The tower was built about 1420, and the church considerably enlarged and altered about 50 years later.

Message book in Dyrham Wood

Cotswold Way ━ ━ ━ ━

Public footpaths - - - - - - -

Viewpoint

For more detail see OS Explorer OL 155

Little
Sodbury

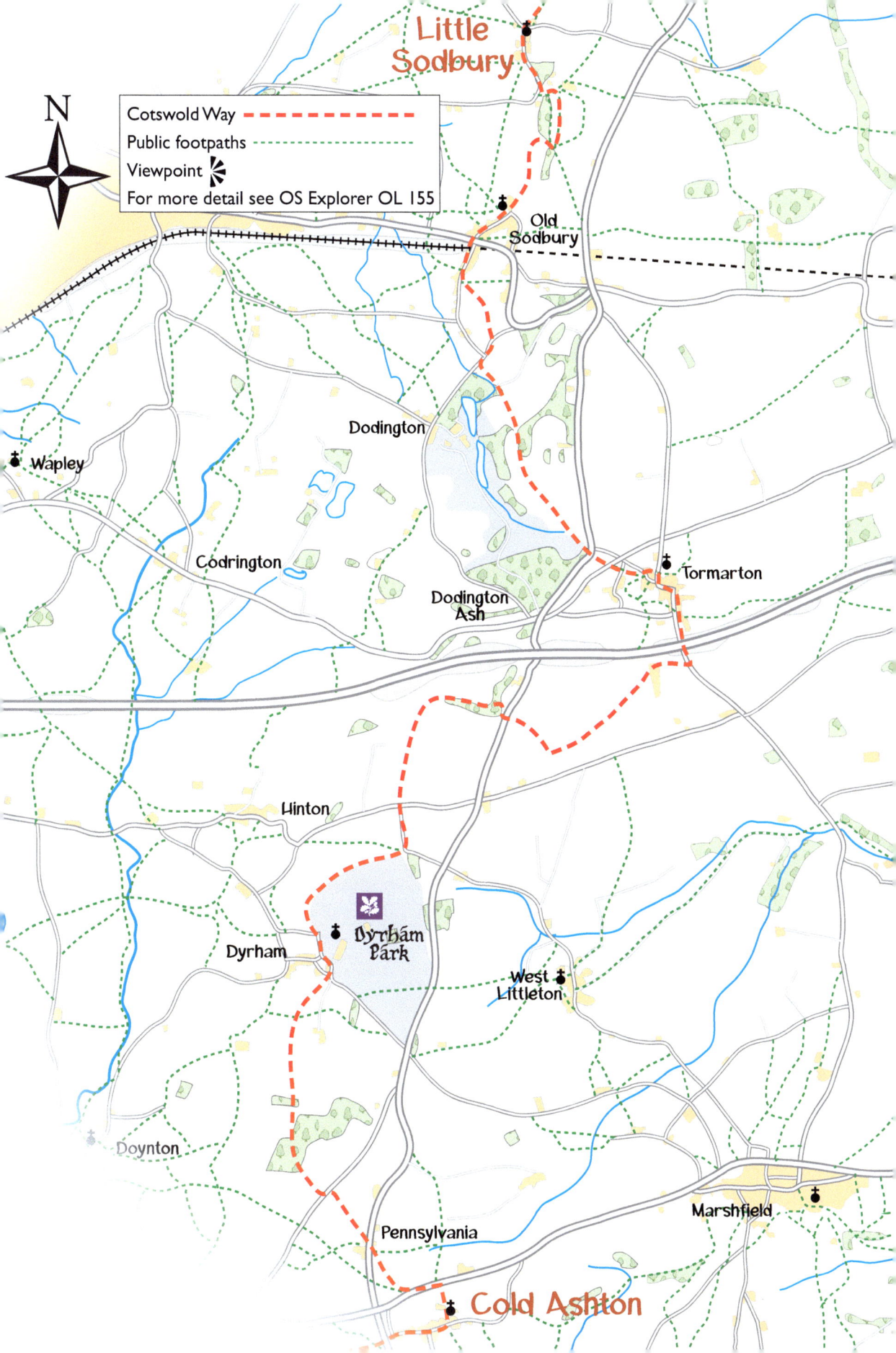

Old
Sodbury

Dodington

Wapley

Codrington

Dodington
Ash

Tormarton

Hinton

Dyrham
Park

Dyrham

West
Littleton

Doynton

Marshfield

Pennsylvania

Cold Ashton

Dyrham Park

As the trail goes through the village, it passes superb ornamental gates through which you can catch sight of the National Trust's Grade I listed Dyrham House. The Wikipedia entry tells us that the house is set in 274 acres (111 ha) of gardens and parkland. The latter had also been home to a herd of 200 fallow deer for centuries. Sadly, however, in early 2021 the herd had to be culled due to the spread of bovine tuberculosis; it's hoped that deer will be re-introduced once the site is declared TB free.

You'll also be pleased to know that the park grounds and gardens are open all year long, with the house also being so on certain days. The car park and main entrance are on the A46 above the house, but walkers along the Cotswold Way can enter through the gate leading to the church and pay the required entrance fee at the shop in the courtyard. It's a 20 minute walk from the car park down the driveway to the house or you can stroll down grassy slopes. Dogs are not permitted in the park, but there is an exercise area for them near the car park.

A good way to make the most of the grounds is to go on one of the guided walks offered by the Park's rangers. The *Park Walk* takes about 45 minutes and is a great opportunity to visit the key viewpoints, enjoy the Cotswold landscape and look across to Wales and the Black Mountains. There are also garden walks pointing out the highlights of the season, with specific walks to introduce visitors to other aspects of the estate. All are free of charge.

The self-guided *Prospect Walk*, says the National Trust, is a 'real must'. Follow the tree-lined avenue from the car park towards Old Lodge and head beyond to the topograph where, on a good day, you can see past the Severn bridges to the Black Mountains in Wales. On the *Journey of Discovery* trail you can spot eight wooden sculptures - including an impressive eagle and subtle snake - taking in the quieter southern side of the park.

As for Dyrham House, you'll find there's a very strong Dutch influence. The west front of 1692 was commissioned from the Huguenot architect, Samuel Hauduroy, and the east front of 1704 from William Talman, architect of Chatsworth. Dyrham also became a showcase of Dutch decorative arts, including delftware, paintings and furniture. 18th century additions include furniture by Gillow and Linnell.

The mastermind behind Dyrham House was William Blathwayt, who was Secretary at War during William and Mary's reign. Blathwayt married the Dyrham heiress, Mary Wynter in 1686 and rebuilt Dyrham Park House between 1692-1704. In the process he is said to have founded a Blathwayt dynasty. Indeed, the Blathwayt family lived at the house until 1956, when the Ministry of Works and National Land Fund bought the manor as a memorial to the WW2 dead. The estate was passed on to the National Trust in 1961. By all accounts, as Lisa Jardine in *BBC News Magazine* reports, Blathwayt was quite a character. The diarist John Evelyn called him 'a very proper person and very dextrous in business', adding 'and has besides all this married a very great fortune'. Old money looked down on him, pronouncing his expenditure on Dyrham Park excessive and unwisely spent: 'My Lord Scarborough thinks he lays out his money not very well'.

Where did all his money come from? Well, suggests Jardine, he was William and Mary's 'imperial fixer'.

> *His successful career was based on the way he could make things happen, at long-distance, throughout English-administered territories, from its American colonies to its farthest-flung tropical island outposts. For this he was handsomely remunerated over a period of 25 years, between the 1680s and the turn of the century. But Blathwayt's salary certainly didn't stretch to cover his magnificent lifestyle at Dyrham Park. That was maintained by systematically extracting backhanders from his "clients".*
>
> *If you want him to act, one of Blathwayt's agents advised the governor of the Island of St Christopher in the Caribbean (now St Kitts), it will cost you. 'Without a gratification of twenty or thirty guineas for himself at least I much doubt the effect of anything else', he wrote. The governor duly sent 30 guineas on behalf of the colony, and added another 10 of his own with an accompanying note: 'To buy you a pair of gloves in acknowledgement of the favour you did me in my business at court'.*

Lisa Jardine also suggests that Blathwayt's way of doing business helps to explain a great deal about the presentation of Dyrham House:

> *The receiving rooms in Blathwayt's mansion are panelled in black walnut, courtesy of the Governor of Maryland. The cypress and cedar wood for the banister and stair risers of the grand main staircase were a gift from the governor of South Carolina, the walnut treads were the contribution of the governor of Virginia. The juniper floorboards came from Jamaica. The extensive gardens, which once boasted some of the most impressive fountains and cascades in England, were planted with exotic foreign plants collected for Blathwayt by colonial officials engaged in business which needed his blessing.*

Apparently, Blathwayt did choose and purchase the Delftware, the ornamental tiles, and splendid Dutch porcelain himself as well as oriental silks and large quantities of tea. This was whenever he accompanied King William to The Hague on royal business. But he made sure that he was charged absolutely no customs duties on them - remonstrating indignantly with anybody who so much as tried.

One thing is for sure. Dyrham Park is a firm favourite as a filming location. Its palmares include the 1993 Merchant Ivory film *The Remains of the Day* (others included Badminton House and Powderham Castle); the 1999 BBC mini-series *Wives and Daughters*; and the 2003, BBC One series *Servants*. An aerial view of Dyrham Park was featured in the opening title sequence of the 2008 film *Australia*. In September 2010, the BBC filmed scenes for the *Doctor Who* sixth series episode *Night Terrors* at Dyrham Park. Dyrham Park was also used for scenes in *The Crimson Field* by the BBC in 2014 and *Sanditon* on ITV in 2019. The BBC series, *Poldark*, filmed scenes at Dyrham Park, as the home of George Warleggan, between 2015 and 2018.

The battle of Deorham - and what it tells us

Dyrham is not just noted for its Park. Just beyond the village is Dyrham Camp, otherwise known as Hinton Hillfort. According to Historic England, it's an example of the 'slight univallate hillfort' type introduced in the Explainer in Chapter 2, i.e. enclosures of various shapes, generally between one and 10ha in size, situated on or close to hilltops and defined by a single line of earthworks, the scale of which is relatively small. Its description goes on:

> *The monument, which falls into two areas of protection, includes a slight univallate hillfort, situated on the summit and tip of a prominent spur called Hinton Hill, overlooking the valleys and confluence of two tributaries to the River Boyd. The hillfort survives as a D-shaped enclosure which measures up to 310m long and 229m wide internally and is defined by a single rampart of up to 10m wide and 2.4m high, with an outer ditch of up to 6m wide and 1.5m deep, which is best preserved to the south and east. To the north, past cultivation and tree growth have reduced the height of the rampart significantly and the associated ditch is largely buried here.*

> *The hillfort was the subject of a limited trial excavation in 1969 when the dimensions of the ramparts were confirmed and the entrance in the centre of the east side was also identified. The hillfort is known by a number of alternative names including 'Dyrham Camp', 'Barhill Camp' or 'Burrills Camp'.*

Hinton Hill is especially significant because it's reckoned to be the site of the Battle of Dyrham (Deorham). To paraphrase Wikipedia, the Anglo-Saxon Chronicle entry for 577 records that in that year King Ceawlin of Wessex and his young son Cuthwine fought the Britons of the West Country at 'the spot that is called Deorham'. The West Saxons carried the day and three kings of the Britons, whose names are given as Conmail, Condidan, and Farinmail, were slain. As a result of the battle, the West Saxons took three important cities, Glevum (Gloucester), Corinium Dobunnorum (Cirencester), and Aquae Sulis (Bath) and so much of Gloucestershire and Worcestershire east of the Severn, along with a small part of northeastern Somerset. In the process, they helped to bring about what came to be known as the Kingdom of Wessex and Alfred the Great fame.

Historians, Wikipedia goes on, are divided on how the battle itself might have unfolded. Some have concluded that the Saxons may have launched a surprise attack and seized the hill fort because it commanded the Avon Valley, and disrupted communications north and south between Bath and her neighbouring Romano-British towns of Gloucester and Cirencester. Once the Saxons were in occupation of the site (and had begun reinforcing the existing Iron Age defensive structures at the site) the Britons of those three towns were compelled to unite and make a combined attempt to dislodge them. Their routed forces were driven north of the River Severn and south of Bath where it appears they began the construction of the defensive earthwork called the Wansdyke in a doomed attempt to prevent more territory from being lost.

The alternative explanation employing the theory of 'Inherent Military Probability' associated with military historian Lieutenant-Colonel Alfred Burne offers a simpler explanation. Ceawlin, it is argued, was methodically advancing towards the Severn and the three forces of Britons concentrated to stop him. Burne suggests that they formed up along two slight ridges across the trackway that skirted the Forest of Braden, with Hinton Hill Camp behind them as their stores depot – a position similar to that adopted at the Battle of Beranburh in AD 556, when the West Saxons are said to have defeated the Britons at Barbury Castle Hill Fort near Swindon. If the Saxon had been able to drive the Britons back from their first line onto the second ridge near the edge of the escarpment, the slightest further retreat would leave their flanks open to a downhill pursuit. He speculates that this is what occurred, with the three Briton leaders and their main body being driven back into the fort while the flanking Saxons driving forwards swept round behind the promontory on which the fort stands. A last stand in this position would explain why none of the three Briton leaders was able to escape.

Either way, it's the date of the battle, 577, and the make-up of its combatants that deserve the attention. The advance of the groups that coalesced to become the West-Saxons, it seems, was much more gradual than is popularly believed - it was nothing like the later Danish or Norman invasions. The first significant Saxon landings in the south of the country had been several generations before 576. It had taken them many years to move westwards to get as far as Dyrham.

A further implication of the events at Dyrham is that Britain didn't totally collapse into the 'dark ages' after the withdrawal of the Roman legions in around 400. As Chapter 2 suggested in highlighting the development of 'rural manors' (Villa Rustica) in the Cotswolds and their on-going survival, Romano-Britain had more substance than it's often given credit for. The battle of Dyrham would appear to confirm this. The local leaders who fought and died there came from the three major cities in the area: Cirencester, which had been a provincial capital in the Roman period, Gloucester or Glevum, a former legionary fortress; and Bath, a renowned spa and religious centre. Getting their act together to confront Ceawlin and his force, even though unsuccessful, surely has to be seen as no mean feat of military intelligence and organisation.

Just outside Dyrham is a memorial seat to Cyril Trenfield. Along with Tony Drake, you will recall from Chapter 1, Cyril helped to create the Cotswold Way in 1971.

Tormarton

The ancient village of Tormarton received its name from the 'tower' (Tor) of the Church, and from Meark, which in Saxon means 'boundary' (i.e. between Mercia and Wessex). It is thought that humans have been active in the area of Tormarton for more than 6000 years. In 1968 the bodies of three Bronze Age men were discovered closeby, when a gas pipeline was being installed. Unusually, two of the bodies showed combat wounds and are now located in Bristol City Museum. Further excavations in 1999 and 2000 found the remains of two other bodies estimated to be 3,500 years old. They are all thought to have all died at a similar time and were then buried in a ditch. A BBC documentary, Meet The Ancestors, was made that followed the second excavation. The area is thought to have been inhabited by the Romans as a stone coffin was found in nearby Hinton. The medieval village was larger than today, extensive earthworks to the north and east of the church suggesting this area may have been settled previously.

The Domesday Book tells that there was a priest at Tormarton, which infers that there was a church here then, dating from Anglo-Saxon days. This AngloSaxon church must have been pulled down in order to build a Norman church of which there remain the 2 lowest stages of the Tower and the Arch and walls of the chancel, and the Tower Arch, all of which are late Norman. The chancel arch has remarkably fine capitals at the head of the pillars and two rows of zigzag. The uppermost stage of the Tower is in the 'Perpendicular' style and dates from the XV century.

Outside the east end of the chancel are two Norman 'string-courses' (raised horizontal hands running round or along the building). The upper one has what is called the 'wheat-ear moulding' and is not found except at Tormarton Church and Norwich Cathedral.

Some historic buildings remain in Tormarton as well as St Mary Magdalene Church, including Manor Farm and Tormarton Court. The Old Manor House was owned by the de la Riviere family, but much of it was demolished in the English Civil War between 1642 and 1649, with only some sections surviving and incorporated into today's Manor Farm. Tormarton Court was constructed in the 18th century. The village became part of the Badminton estate owned by the Duke of Beaufort in 1789. In 1848 the population of the parish was 620 but is now barely half this number.

As you cross over the A46 near Tormarton (at ST 76302 79000), you'll notice that the milestone shows this was a turnpike road. It also says 10 miles to Bath even though Cotswold Way walkers have already done 17 miles!

Dodington - the second grand estate

The second estate you pass through, Dodington, is in private hands (those of James Dyson, the inventor of the vacuum cleaner that bears his name) and is pretty much like walking through the normal countryside. It's nonetheless been meticulously restored to the grand estate it once was, one thing to note, especially near Tormarton, being the several miles of renewed dry stone walls. It's not something that's seen very often these days.

According to Historic England, at the time of the Domesday survey, the manor of Dodington belonged to the family of Berkeley of Dursley and a medieval building existed on the site of what is now the lower lake. The Berkeley line ended in 1382 and the estate came by marriage into the Wekys family, who built a new manor house before selling it on to Giles Codrington in the late 1600s.

The estate was bought from his relatives by General Christopher Codrington, governor of the Leeward Islands in c 1700. Wikipedia tells us that there were no fewer than three Christopher Codringtons - son, father and grandfather. All were involved at different times in running the Codrington Plantations, which were two historic sugarcane producing estates on the island of Barbados. Like many plantations of the period, they were heavily dependent on slavery.

In 1712, Atkyns notes that Sir William Codrington, the General's son, 'hath a large house near the Church, and very large and beautiful gardens, and a great Estate in this Parish' (Atkyns 1712). The title of baronet was granted to the Codringtons of Dodington in 1721. Alexander Pope visited in 1728 and described the house as, 'pretty enough, the situation romantic, covered with woody hills, stumbling upon one another confusedly, and the garden makes a valley between them with some mounts and waterfalls'. The landscape park was laid out around 1764 by Capability Brown for Sir William

Codrington. It was modified in 1793 by Emes and J Webb for Christopher Bethell Codrington. A formal garden was added in 1930. The estate remained in the Codrington family until 1980.

There has also recently been a fallout from the Codringtons' association with slavery. As well as the Dodington estate and its house, one of the beneficiaries of the Codrington wealth was the library of the same name at All Souls, Oxford. In January 2021, the name was removed from the library due to his association with slave labour and a plaque placed outside commemorating those who worked on the Codrington plantations.

One thing to note as you cross the Dodington Estate, especially near Tormarton, is that Sir James Dyson, its owner, has renewed many miles of dry stone walls. It's not something that's seen very often these days.

How's this for a dry stone wall - on the Dodington estate

By kind permission of Richard Wilson

The Sodburys and their hill fort

If you look at the OS map, you'll see there are no fewer than three Sodburys: the much bigger market town of Chipping Sodbury to the west and Sodbury and Little Sodbury on the trail itself. The name is recorded in Anglo-Saxon (in the dative case) as Soppanbyrig = 'Soppa's fort' and in Domesday Book as Sopeberie. The name probably refers to the Iron Age hillfort just to the north-east of the village that you will be introduced to shortly.

On the escarpment immediately above and to the east of Sodbury/Old Sodbury village, and visible from the main road, is a crenellated tower resembling a rook chess piece. It performs the function of a ventilation shaft (the first of six) for the Chipping Sodbury Tunnel on the main railway line from South Wales, via Bristol Parkway, to London Paddington. This line was opened in 1903 as part of the Great Western Railway, which runs through the village and under the hill above it. Trains used to stop at Chipping Sodbury and Badminton stations, which were closed following the Beeching cuts. The nearest station is now Yate on the main line from Bristol Temple Meads to Birmingham, which separates from the former Great Western Railway at Westerleigh, to the South of Yate.

The tunnel is 2.5 miles (four kms) long and cost £0.25 million. Constructed between 1897-1903, the first sod was cut in 1897 by the Duchess of Beaufort. Brick Kiln Field (west of Chapel Lane) produced 18.5million bricks using a boiler that was brought down from the Forth Railway Bridge. Bricks were taken up to the ventilator shafts by overhead rail over Chapel Lane and Badminton Road. (There is an old photo of this overhead line decorated for the visit of the Prince and Princess of Wales in 1902).

The Church of Saint John the Baptist above Old Sodbury is of late Norman period, and although it has been enlarged and altered, much of the original work remains. In the nave there is an arcade of Norman columns, there are two Norman windows and the tower is also Norman. It also has two effigies of knights: one is late 14th century, carved in wood; and the other is dated to 1240, carved in stone, featuring a very large shield. These two are considered to have been lords of the local manor.

In the churchyard at Old Sodbury are a number of old bale-tombs occupied by rich merchants. Some of the gravestones date back to the early 19th century. Look out, too, for the interpretation board at the end of Chapel Lane. Designed by the local Cotswold Wardens, this gives a description of the many features of interest in Old Sodbury.

Also worth a mention is Catchpott Lane. Once upon a time there was a turnpike road here (now A432) and a toll house. The lane is so named because a lad was put there with a pot to catch people trying to avoid paying at the tollhouse.

You might also like to know that Old Sodbury is the starting point of a couple of walks you might do sometime: The Frome Valley Walkway follows the river of that name to Bristol and Jubilee Way that goes to the old River Severn Crossing at Aust.

As the trail goes towards Little Sodbury, you'll see on your right your second hillfort of the stage and the third since leaving Bath. Historic England refers to Old Sodbury Hillfort, as it's come to be named, in the following terms:

> *The monument includes a large multivallate hillfort, situated on the summit of a small ridge on a plateau forming part of the Cotswold Escarpment, overlooking the wide valley of the River Frome. The hillfort survives as a roughly rectangular enclosed area, defined by a widely-spaced double rampart and ditch on all except the western side, where there is a single rampart and berm above the escarpment, and to the east where there is an additional outer counterscarp bank. In total the hillfort covers approximately 9.48ha, and the interior measures up to 277m long by 190m wide. The inner rampart, present on all sides, survives differentially, but measures up to 10m wide and 2.1m high. It is surrounded by a ditch of up to 9m wide and 2.1m deep (except to the west) with a further berm of up to 6m wide. The outer rampart is present to the north, east and south, again surviving differentially, and measures up to 17m wide and 3m high with a 3.6m wide berm and an outer ditch of up to 13m wide and 3m deep. The interior is crossed by a slight bank and ditch which is the parish boundary bank. The hillfort was once thought to have been a Roman camp which could have held up to five cohorts of soldiers and their horse soldiers. It is now widely accepted as an Iron Age hillfort.*

The fort's location is reckoned to be a mystery due to its relative difficulty in access and lack of fresh water supplies locally, but is thought to be connected with the much ruined Horton hill fort a couple of miles to the north. It certainly has commanding views of the Frome Valley, Severn Vale and the Welsh mountains. The Romans are thought to have strengthened the fort for use as a camp to support their western frontier. In AD 577 the Saxon army are also believed to have used the fort as a camp before the battle of Dyrham, a few miles to the south. It was almost certainly also used during the wars of the roses.

Although the fort is in private hands, it is accessible and can be reached by footpath from the A46 road and through the village from below via the Cotswold Way. It's also a location where you'll find signs of the work of the Cotswold Voluntary Wardens: they've done a lot of clearing of scrub trees in order to preserve the historic features of the area and return it to limestone grassland.

Just beyond the hillfort is Little Sodbury village - a tiny collection of houses, with a pretty church and a manor house, and one of three 'Thankful Villages' in Gloucestershire, i.e. rare places that suffered no fatalities during WW1. Little Sodbury Manor nestles on the slope immediately next to the fort. It had a chapel (uniquely) dedicated to St Aveline. In the 15th century it was also the home of Sir John Walsh who employed William Tyndale to whom the Tyndale Monument is dedicated as chaplain and tutor to his grandchildren in 1522-3; by tradition Tynedale began his translation of the Bible in his bedroom here as well as preaching in the chapel. The manor retains the porch and Great Hall of the fifteenth-century courtyard house, with a timber roof resting on corbels carved as shield bearing angels The house fell into disrepair in the nineteenth century, but was restored by architect Sir Harold Brakspear for Lord Grosvenor and later Baron de Tuyll.

St Adeline's Church has the distinction of being the only church in the United Kingdom named after St. Adeline, an Abbess of the Benedictine order who died in 1125. The current church was built in 1859 by William James and said to incorporate parts of the former church which stood near the manor. It also as far as possible followed the design of its predecessor at the Manor, being in in the 'Perpendicular' style, consisting of nave (without chancel), north aisle, vestry, south porch and an embattled south-western tower with pinnacles, containing the old bell. There are 150 sittings.

The reason for rebuilding the church, it seems, is that there was no burial ground in the parish. 'It had no graveyard—the hard rock of the terrace resisting all efforts of pick or shovel. This necessitated burial at the mother church of Old Sodbury, a mile or so away across the fields; and more than once in winter time, as the mourners were lifting their burden over the ice-coated stiles en route, the coffin slipped and fell, with gruesome results. The site was therefore abandoned and the new church built at the foot of the hill in 1859'.

Cotswold Way Circular Walk

Old Sodbury is the location of one of the twelve Cotswold Way Circular Walks. It's No 11 and entitled 'Old Sodbury – The Hill Fort and Church'. In the words of the National Trails website:

'From the delightful village of Old Sodbury, follow the Cotswold Way up to the serenity of a medieval church, around oak-fringed farmland and along shaded paths to the breath-taking outcrop of an iron-age hillfort. Views, history, peace and rest all combine to make this simple little stroll a wonderful taster of the southern Cotswolds'.

- Distance: 2½ miles. Duration: 1½ – 2 hours. Difficulty: Easy to moderate – no stiles, steepish slopes'.
- You can download the map from www.nationaltrail.co.uk

Car Parking
- For the start in Cold Ashton, see the end point on the previous stage.
- Parking in Little Sodbury is very limited. Try the Lane just beyond the church. Old Sodbury is your alternative.

Chapter 5
Into wool country
Little Sodbury to Wotton-under-Edge

You'll find subtle changes on this stage. The trail gives you fewer views to the east from the escarpment and more to the west. The landscape is also slightly different. The trail passes through woodland as well as open pasture and arable farmland. The built environment is also different. The stage has its share of manor houses in the hands of the National Trust as well as an outstanding monument, but the houses aren't quite on the scale of Dyrham and Dodington. Clearer, too, on this stage is the significance of wool to the Cotswolds. There are few signs of mills these days, although there is one that's still in working order. Yet the legacy of mill owner houses is there in even the smallest village. You'll also be passing through one of the larger towns to be found on the trail and one of several that might be said to be built on wool.

Horton

Just after Little Sodbury, the Cotswolds Way is joined by the Monarch's Way as it comes from Chipping Sodbury on the left. As Chapter 2 has pointed out, the Monarch's Way is a 615 mile (990 kms) long distance path that approximates the escape route taken by the future King Charles II in 1651 after being defeated in the Battle of Worcester. It runs from Worcester via Bristol and Yeovil to Brighton. The waymarks are yellow and show a picture of a ship above the Prince of Wales' three-point feathered crown superimposed on a Royal Oak tree (which is at Boscobel House) in black. The ship is the *Surprise* and was originally a coal brig, becoming the HMY Royal Escape when Charles 2 returned from France to become King at the Restoration in 1660. The Cotswold Way and Monarch's Way part company for a short stretch at the Somerset Monument, meet up again at Lower Kilcott and take final leave of one another near Kilcott Mill.

Another mile or so brings you to Horton. The name is a common one in England. It normally derives from Old English horu ('dirt') and tun ('settlement, farm, estate'), presumably meaning 'farm on muddy soil'. This small settlement, nestling below the Cotswold escarpment, is highly picturesque in its setting. The small numbers of buildings that make up the settlement create its unique charm especially with the use of local Cotswold stone.

Just north of the village, near Horton Court, is the Parish Church of St James the Elder. 12th century in origin and predominantly perpendicular in style, it was rebuilt in the 14th century and altered in the 15th and 16th centuries. It was further restored in 1865. The church still retains a Norman font and Jacobean pulpit. Almost immediately after, you will come across 'The Castles', which is a 'univallate promontory fort'. In the words of Historic England,

> *The monument includes a promontory fort, situated on the summit of a projecting spur, overlooking the valley of the Little Avon River. The fort survives as a roughly D-shaped enclosure defined to the north and east by a curving single rampart and buried ditch. It is defined to the remaining sides by steep natural scarp slopes, augmented partially to the south by a short*

N

Wotton-Under-Edge

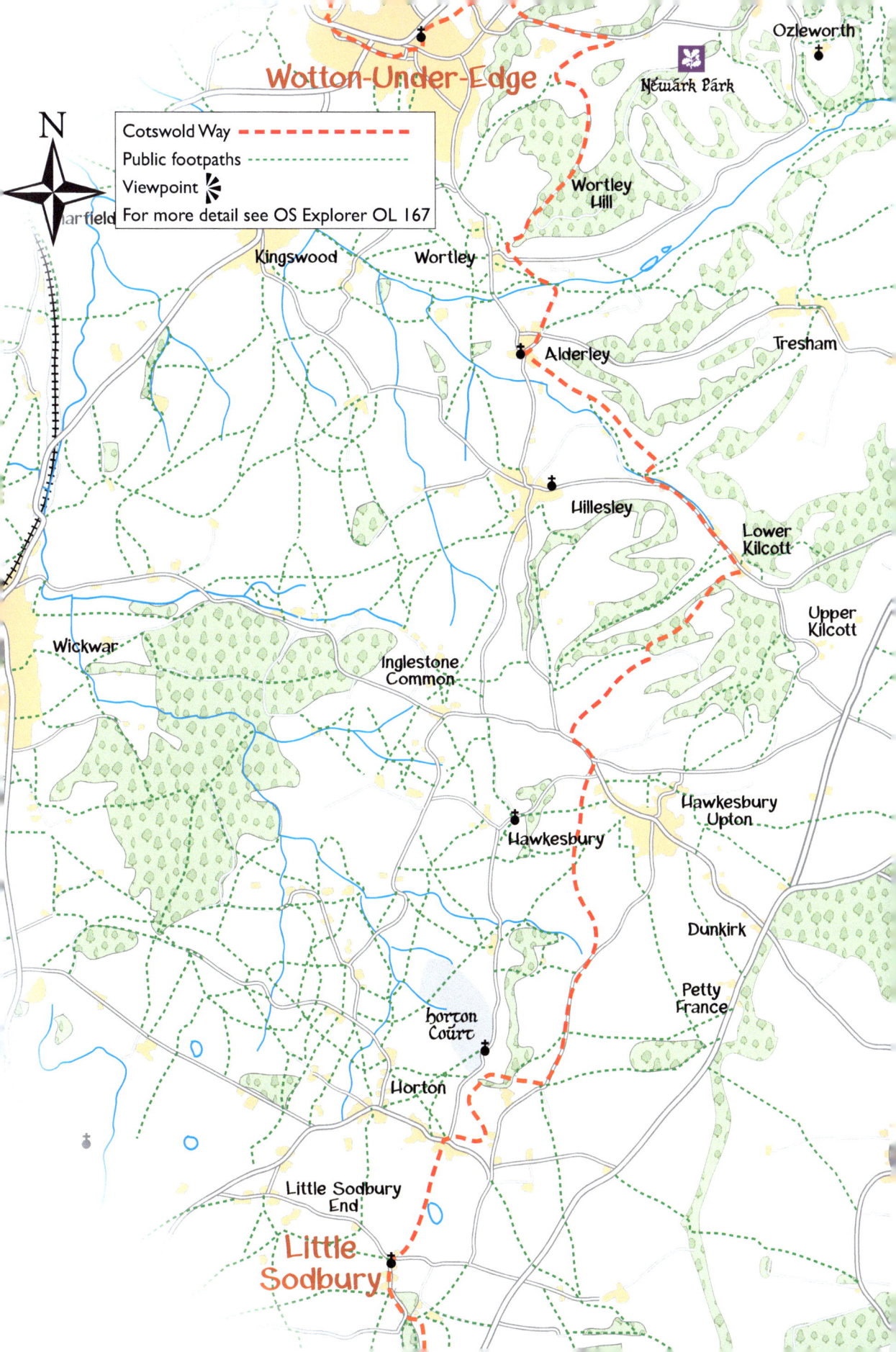

Ozleworth

Newark Park

Wortley Hill

Kingswood

Wortley

Tresham

Alderley

Hillesley

Lower Kilcott

Upper Kilcott

Wickwar

Inglestone Common

Hawkesbury Upton

Hawkesbury

Dunkirk

Petty France

horton Court

Horton

Little Sodbury End

Little Sodbury

length of slight rampart bank. The interior of the promontory fort measures up to a maximum of 203m long by 158m wide and the whole covers approximately 2.78ha. The partial southern rampart bank is up to 0.6m high whilst the main north and eastern rampart bank is up to 12.1m wide and 3m high. Exposed limestone in this area appears to show evidence for fire reddening. The ditch, which measures up to 7.2m wide, is buried and generally the soil is of a darker hue and stone free. Two or even three possible entrances have been identified, including one to the east, but none are conclusively original. The fort is known locally as 'Horton Camp' or 'The Castles'.

Historic England goes on to explain that promontory forts are 'broadly contemporary with other types of hillfort …[but] are regarded as settlements of high status … their construction and choice of location [having] as much to do with display as defence'. Apparently, promontory forts are rare with less than 100 recorded examples.

Just beyond the fort is Horton Court with fine views of it from the trail as it rises above the escarpment. This is a Grade I listed manor house that's been in the hands of the National Trust since 1949, following the death in 1946 of Miss Hilda Proctor Wills, who was a member of the Bristol-based

Horton Court

The National Trust's Horton Court

Imperial Tobacco Company of Bristol. She bequeathed the property to the National Trust in memory of her thirty three year old nephew of the Coldstream Guards, killed in action in Italy in 1945.

The Horton Court estate is reputed to have at one time been owned by one of King Harold's sons. The oldest part of the house was built as a rectory by Robert de Beaufeu, who was rector of Horton and prebendary of Salisbury. The Norman doorways and windows have rounded arches and the roof is arch-braced and dates to the fourteenth century. It's said to be one of the oldest houses in the country, with parts of the great hall and north wing dating from 1140, with further additions to the north wing added in the fourteenth, fifteenth and eighteenth centuries. The rest of the house was built in 1521 for William Knight, who was later the Bishop of Bath and Wells and Chief Secretary to Henry V111. The house has an L-shaped plan and is constructed of stone with a stone slate roof.

Britain Express suggests that what makes Horton Court so intriguing is that it is one of the very few examples of an unfortified Norman domestic building in the country. Normally, the Normans built with defence firmly in mind, so domestic buildings were well fortified and might better resemble a castle than a house. Horton Court, on the other hand, seems to have escaped this approach entirely.

Horton Court has been used as a filming location for both *Wolf Hall* and *Poldark*. It is available to members of the public as a holiday let, but is unfortunately not open to the public.

Between the Hawkesburys

The trail now wends its way between two Hawkesburys. To the left is plain 'Hawkesbury', which is a small cluster of houses and to the right the larger 'Hawkesbury Upton" ('upp Tunn' or 'upper enclosure'). Hawkesbury Upton, which is close to the A46 road, exhibits many of the characteristics of a typical Cotswold village, including use of the local limestone in the majority of the buildings. The village has two pubs - the Beaufort Arms and the Fox Inn, both on the High Street - a primary school, a village shop, a post office and a hair salon. There is also a village hall with a recreation ground and a cricket club.

Hawkesbury was a rural parish in which agriculture and animal husbandry were economically dominant. The climate in southwestern Gloucestershire was partial to raising potatoes, apparently, along with domesticated animals. Cattle and sheep were important to the livelihood of the residents of Hawkesbury as there was a fair held on last Friday in August for the sale of those animals. The raising of sheep was a principal source of income, primarily for their wool. Homes constructed along streams aided in the wool production industry as it provided water necessary for dying and washing. This water also provided means to grind corn in grist mills and finish cloth in fulling mills.

On the last Saturday in August, the annual Hawkesbury Horticultural Show takes place at the village hall and recreation ground. The show features a large marquee, where the best fruit, vegetables and flowers, as well as home baking, varied crafts, home made wine and beer, original photographs and pictures are exhibited – all produced by the local community. In addition, there is entertainment in the arena, a carnival procession, fairground rides and a wide range of local craft, trade and charity stalls. The show has been running continuously since 1885 - never once cancelled for adverse weather or war - something which villagers are extremely proud of. Sadly, the 2020 show was postponed due to COVID.

You might like to know that the research for this book has raised a query that so far hasn't been answered. It involves a deserted brick building in the coroner of one of the fields between Horton and Hawkesbury Upton. Inside there are two spaces: the smaller might have housed a generator; the larger was perhaps used as a shelter or accommodation. It may be a legacy from WW2, but the local Cotswold Wardens have so far been unable to confirm. Answers please to support@ cotswoldwayassociation.org.uk.

A short distance from Hawkesbury Upton on the road towards Hillesley, and almost appearing out of nowhere, is the Somerset Monument. It takes the form of a slightly tapering square tower, about 100 feet (30 metres) high and can be seen from the Tyndale Monument at North Nibley. Built in ashlar stone and designed by Lewis Vulliamy, it was constructed in 1846 as a memorial to Lord Edward Somerset, who led the British cavalry at the Battle of Waterloo. The story goes that Lord Edward, who was a nephew of the Sixth Duke of Beaufort from closeby Badminton, lost his hat during the first cavalry charge and in the subsequent search for it a cannonball tore off the flap of his coat and killed his horse. He was awarded a GCB in 1834. The tower is currently closed - there was hope that the viewing platform might be reopened for the 50th Anniversary celebration of the Cotswold Way, but at the time of writing this looked unlikely.

Wikipedia tells us that the first keeper of the monument was Shadrack Byfield, who lived in Hawkesbury Upton from 1843 to 1856. Shadrack's claim to fame is that he was a one-armed veteran of the Anglo-

American War of 1812 and the author of a memoir of his wartime experiences, *A Narrative of a Light Company Soldier's Service*, published in 1840. Apparently, this work is one of the few accounts of the conflict penned by a common British soldier.

Kilcott mill

One of the first indications of coming into wool country will be found just along from the monument. It's Kilcott Mill, which was built in the late 1600s and altered and extended in the 18th and 19th centuries. Just east of the village of Hillesley, it was one of many mills that used to operate in South Gloucestershire, several being located down the valley at quarter of a mile intervals - this distance, it's said, was the closest practical spacing to provide a sufficient head water to turn a water wheel. Killcott Mill still has its mill pond, sluice and related buildings, with its water wheel inside to prevent freezing up in winter.

Today it is believed to be the only mill in that area still using its historic machinery driven by water. The water supply comes from the Kilcott Brook, which rises just over a mile upstream out of springs from the Cotswold escarpment. The flow is not what it used to be, but is just enough to restore the level of the mill pool after grinding for an hour or two.

Kilcott Mill has a long history. The first record of a mill was in the Domesday Book of 1086, which listed Hawkesbury as having three mills of an annual value of nineteen shillings and two pence. Enquiries from local Cotswold Wardens at the Gloucestershire Records Office have yielded a wealth of information about the property. The mill itself was rebuilt in 1655 and many later alterations can clearly be distinguished. In 1677 the present mill house was built as a separate dwelling and remains, except for the installation of sanitation, electricity and water, as it used to be. Every effort has been made to preserve features such as internal window shutters, fan- lights, built-in clothes closets and stone flagged floors. In the mill, the same policy has been followed, and repairs and restoration have faithfully followed previous patterns and styles.

Alderley

Next up is Alderley. The village, reports Wikipedia, has an entry in the Domesday Book of 1086, where it is referred to as 'Alrelie' meaning, perhaps not surprisingly, 'woodland clearing where alders grow'. It is recorded as being located in the hundred of Grimboldestou with a total population of 16 households (7 villagers, 5 smallholders, 4 slaves), while also boasting 2 lord's plough teams, 7 men's plough teams, 12 acres of meadows and a mill. By the 16th and 17th centuries, the number of woollen mills had grown considerably. In 1779 Samuel Rudder's *A New History of Gloucestershire* states that Alderley had been home to the clothing industry for hundreds of years.

The parish church is dedicated to St Kenelm. Kenelm, you may remember from Chapter 2, was an 8th-century king and member of the Mercian royal family. He was murdered by a relative, but according to legend a spring burst forth where he was buried, and the water gave healing properties. He was carried by monks to Winchcombe, where his shrine was a popular place of pilgrimage throughout the medieval period. If there is such a thing as a local Cotswold saint, Kenelm is it. The oldest part of St Kenelm's church is the 14th-century tower, but the rest of the building was rebuilt in the Victorian period.

Near the church is Alderley House. The house stands on the site of a Jacobean manor built by the barrister, lawyer, and judge Sir Matthew Hale from 1656. Hale is best known for his treatise *Historia Placitorum Coronae* or *The History of the Pleas of the Crown*. In an age when corruption was common, Hale was also known for his honesty and willingness to make politically incorrect decisions if they upheld the law. As the Wikipedia entry tells us, the house, or rather houses because there was a Lower and Upper House, has been rebuilt on several occasions, the latest version being constructed in the mid-1900s. The house served as a school after WWII but is now a private dwelling.

A sunken lane near Wortley Hill

Wortley and the approach to Wotton-under-Edge

The village of Wortley is very quiet now. Once upon a time, though, it was a Manor held by Henry VIII in 1544 and by Elizabeth in 1572. In later times, Wortley lay at the centre of what was a high concentration of fulling mills operating in the valley. Many 17th and early 18th century clothiers lived in houses near their mills, their gabled dwellings looking much like some of the adjacent mills, as wealth was accumulated. Houses were remodelled and some clothiers moved away from the valleys to live in grander, more spacious houses on the hillsides. When Wortley house, formerly the home of the Osborne family of Monks mill, Alderley, was advertised for sale in 1776, it was said to be 'fit for a gentleman or a Clothier'.

Wortley has also been in the spotlight more recently for other reasons, the site of a hitherto unknown Roman Villa being discovered. Apparently, the landowner, Paul Cory, was digging a hole for a fence post in 1981 when he stumbled on it, coming up with some mosaic flooring and pieces of painted wall plaster. Some local enthusiasts opened a trench which revealed the badly-damaged pilae of a hypocaust system of parts of two rooms of a bathhouse, together with considerable quantities of painted wall plaster, tesserae and tegulae, some pottery and bone. In 1983 the site was taken over, at the request of Mr Cory, by the University of Keele as a training excavation for students from not only England but from various parts of the world as well. Wortley continued to be a training excavation site until 1996. The uniqueness of the Wortley site lies in two of its structures: its cellar and its bathhouse.

Look at the map and you might wonder why the trail from Wortley takes such a roundabout route to get into Wotton. The reason is that it's so much more scenic than the direct route. After Wortley, you go up the hill of the same name where you'll have high banks on either side in some places. On your left, you'll also get glimpses of the wonderfully named 'Nanny Farmer's Bottom'. 'Bottom', it seems, is a favourite adjective to describe the many side valleys in the area - as well as Nanny Farmer's, there are also Muscovy, Ozleworth and Tyley 'Bottoms'.

A second reason is that there's much ancient and modern interest. Blackberries Hill long barrow is the most ancient. Historic England describes it like this:

The monument includes a long cairn situated on the summit of an extremely prominent ridge which forms the watershed between the valleys of the Marlees Brook and a tributary to the Little Avon River. Known locally as 'The Clump' this long cairn survives as a rectangular stony mound aligned north east to south west. It measures approximately 39.6m long, 18.2m wide and up to 1.5m high with its side ditches preserved as buried features. The mound has an uneven profile as a result of the early partial excavation, stone robbing and past tree growth. It is surrounded by a drystone wall and has been recently cleared of trees and scrubby vegetation.

The route also takes you to the edge of the National Trust's Newark Park Estate, which you can reach by a lane as the trail turns onto Blackquarries Hill. At the centre of the estate of some 700 acres (2.8 km2) is a Grade I listed country house of Tudor origins built between 1544 and 1556 as a hunting lodge for Sir Nicholas of the Poyntz family using stones from Kingswood Abbey further north. It was added to in the 1790s and later converted into a fashionable Georgian home.

Close by also is the wonderfully named village of Ozleworth. Here St Nicholas of Myra's Church is unusual on two counts: it is one of only two churches in Gloucestershire with a hexagonal tower and the churchyard is circular. The Ozleworth estate is currently owned by the Stone family.

St. Nicholas of Myra Church

Wotton-under-Edge

The modern interest is Wotton-under-Edge's own BT tower. 76.2 metres (250 ft) tall, it's said to be one of the country's few telecommunication towers built of reinforced concrete.

As the Wotton-under-Edge Historical Society's timeline tells us, the first record of Wotton is in an Anglo-Saxon Royal Charter of King Edmund I, who in AD 940 leased four hides of land in Wudetun to Eadric. The name Wudetun means the 'enclosure, homestead or village' (tun) in or near the wood (wude). The 'Edge', as Chapter 2 explained, refers to the limestone escarpment of the Cotswold Edge which includes the hills of Wotton Hill and Tor Hill that flank the town. 'Edge' has also become a term used by locals to describe the area.

Wotton-under-Edge - a town built on wool

Much of the character of present day Wotton reflects its key role in the wool trade in the early middle ages, like Painswick and Chipping Campden further along the trail. There's the 13th century market place area known as the 'Chipping', which used to attract wool buyers from far and wide - including from Flanders and Italy. There's also the church, St. Mary the Virgin, which you pass on your way in and which was consecrated in 1283; most of the church as it is today was probably completed in 1325.

The church is perhaps best known not so much for its architecture, however, but for its large organ. Positioned in the south-east corner of the church, adjacent to the altar, it is said to be one of the biggest organs in the county and is famed for having been played by George Handel when in its previous location of St Martin in the Fields in London. For those interested in organ architecture, it's said to possess a large range of stops over three manuals and a pedalboard, including two trumpets, six diapasons, a cornopean, and a flute ...

Most definitely an example of medieval architecture is the former public house known as the Ancient

Ram Inn. The inn has been owned by many people since 1145, when it was first established, and has been most recently in the hands of the Humphries family. Reputedly, the Inn is one of the ten most haunted places in England. It has also been investigated by many paranormal researchers, particularly for television shows like *Ghost Adventures and Most Haunted Great British Ghosts*. It's also featured on TV in Canada, Denmark and Sweden. The Ghost Club investigated the inn in 2003, but didn't register anything paranormal.

A key influence on Wotton's early involvement in the wool trade was the Cistercian Abbey of Kingswood just a mile and a half away (2.5kms). Established in 1139, the abbey was demolished at the time of Dissolution of the Monasteries in the 1530s and all that remains is the Grade 1 listed gate house. In earlier times, however, it was renowned for its sheep rearing expertise and had connections across Europe.

Also important was the powerful Berkely family whose famous castle is just a few miles to the north west: Wotton was a dependency of the manor of Berkeley. It was William of Berkeley who invited the Cistercians to come to Wotton in 1139. It was Johanna de Berkeley who was given a charter in 1252 to hold a market in Wotton, along with a three-day annual fair on the Feast of the Cross; Borough status followed in 1253. It was Katherine Lady Berkeley who in 1384 founded the grammar school that still bears her name.

With the decline in the wool trade, Wotton made a successful transition into cloth making, exploiting the local fast flowing streams for powering fulling mills and the dyeing process as well as locally dug fullers' earth. Much of the famous red cloth of which the uniforms of the British army were made in the 1700s and early 1800s was produced locally and sold to the British as well as foreign governments. The red cloth was favoured because it was the cheapest material made. Another period of prosperity reached its peak in the 17th and 18th centuries and is reflected in its many Jacobean and Georgian properties.

Especially notable are the almshouses in Church Street. As *Cotswolds Info* tells us:

There are three groups of Almshouses, evidence of Wotton's concern for the aged, and all of which continue in use today. The earliest of these is one of the most notable examples in the town of traditional Cotswold stone building. Hugh Perry in the 17th century and Thomas Dawes in the 18th were responsible for the Almshouses which bear their names in Church Street. The first buildings were erected in 1638 as a result of a bequest by Hugh Perry, with accommodation for six poor men and six poor women. The building has six gables facing the street and a central domed wooden cupola. A flat-arched passageway leads into a courtyard in which is situated a beautiful, tiny 17th century chapel. The 'Dawes hospital' of 1720 completes the rectangle on the east side. Visitors are welcome to enter this quiet enclosure, which 'seems like an Oxford college in miniature' (David Verey).

The second row of almshouses was founded by Miss Ann Bearpacker in 1837. They stand in two groups of five opposite the parish church, next to Parklands. An extensive programme of restoration and modernisation has just been completed, making them suitable for continued use into the 21st century but without losing anything of their traditional appearance. The Rowland Hill Almshouses, with their wooden verandas, founded in 1887 in memory of the Rev. Rowland Hill, may be seen just below the Tabernacle in Tabernacle Pitch at the top of Old Town.

One of Wotton's more recent claims to fame is that Sir Isaac Pitman, inventor of Pitman shorthand, moved to Wotton in 1836 after training as a teacher. He lived in Orchard Street, a small side road off Long Street, where there is a plaque on the house he occupied. He started his own school and spent three years in Wotton before moving to Bath in 1839. Most of his development of shorthand would seem to have been done in Wotton - his system of phonetic shorthand was first published in 1837 in a pamphlet titled *Sound-Hand*. In 1886 Pitman went into partnership with his sons, Alfred and Ernest, to form Isaac Pitman and Sons, which was to become one of the world's leading educational publishers and training businesses with offices across the world. In the early 1970s a housing estate in Wotton, Pitman Place, was named in his honour.

An even more recent claim to fame is the setting up of one of the first (if not the first) all-digital Cinemas in the UK. In 2002, following the closure of the local Cinema, a group of volunteers got together and raised funds for a replacement. Opened in 2005, the Wotton Electric Picture House is a 100 seat modern facility inside an old stable yard that was once part of the Crown Inn.

Wotton's alm houses in Church Street

Cotswold Way Circular Walk

Wotton-under-Edge is the location of one of the twelve Cotswold Way Circular Walks. It's No 10. In the words of the National Trails website:

'As rich farmland gives way to woodland tracks and rolling parkland, this enchanting walk leads you from scarp top to valley bottom, back into one of the Cotswolds' most charming and thriving small towns. With spectacular views, intriguing shops and historic architecture, all tastes will find something wonderful in this special little corner of the Cotswolds.

- Distance: 5 miles (6½ with detour to Newark Park). Duration: 3 – 4 hours (4 – 5 hours with detour). Difficulty: Moderate – Stiles and steep sections'.
- You can download the map from www.nationaltrail.co.uk

Car Parking

- For the start in Little Sodbury, see the end point on the previous stage.
- In Wotton-under-Edge, there is long stay parking at 'The Chipping' in Sym Lane (GL12 7AD) and at the Civic Centre on Gloucester Street (GL12 7DN).

Look out for the Monarch's Way

Chapter 6
A landmark visible for miles
Wotton-under-Edge to Cam Peak

Like a lot of the Cotswold Way as it heads northwards, this stage has a good mixture of views, woods and valleys. The beech woods provide an especially fantastic colour show in autumn. There's another hill fort, which is in pretty pristine condition. There's also a major example of benefaction which helps the public to enjoy the Cotswolds' highlights. Towards the end, you pass through the largest and most industrial town on the Cotswold Way, which is steeped in engineering as well as cloth making history. You then climb up a famous hill that is actually called a 'peak'. Above all, you have the pleasure of coming face to face with perhaps the most iconic monument on the Cotswold Way: it really can be seen for miles - including from the M5 when you should have your eyes on the road.

Brackenbury Ditches

The trail takes you out of Wotton on the most direct route possible down the High Street followed by a climb up Wotton Hill. As well as getting you into your stride, this will give you yet more wonderful views. You might also like to know that much of the hill is a Site of Special Scientific Interest (SSSI) on account of its biology as well as geology - it's owned and managed by the National Trust and the Gloucestershire Wildlife Trust. You will also pass a small walled enclosure with an emblematic cluster of pine trees, which can be spotted from the town as you go up. Sometimes known as the 'Clump', a collection of trees has been there since the early 19th century. Initially, the trees commemorated the Battle of Waterloo and then were replaced at the time of Victoria's Golden Jubilee in 1887. The spot is also said to have housed one of the early beacons used to warn of the approach of the Spanish Armada in 1588.

Before you realise it, you will have arrived at your second point of interest. It's a monument known as 'Brackenbury Ditches' (or, sometimes, 'Beckett's Bury') on the side of Westbridge Wood. British History Online notes that Brackenbury Ditches, which lies in woodland, is the only hill-fort wholly untouched by ploughing or quarrying. In the words of Historic England:

> *This monument includes a slight univallate hillfort with outworks situated on a natural promontory on the Cotswold Escarpment overlooking the wide valley of the Doverte Brook. The hillfort survives as a roughly triangular enclosure defined on two sides by a simple rampart bank measuring up to 15.2m wide and 3m high above the natural steep scarp slopes and*

Brackenbury Ditches

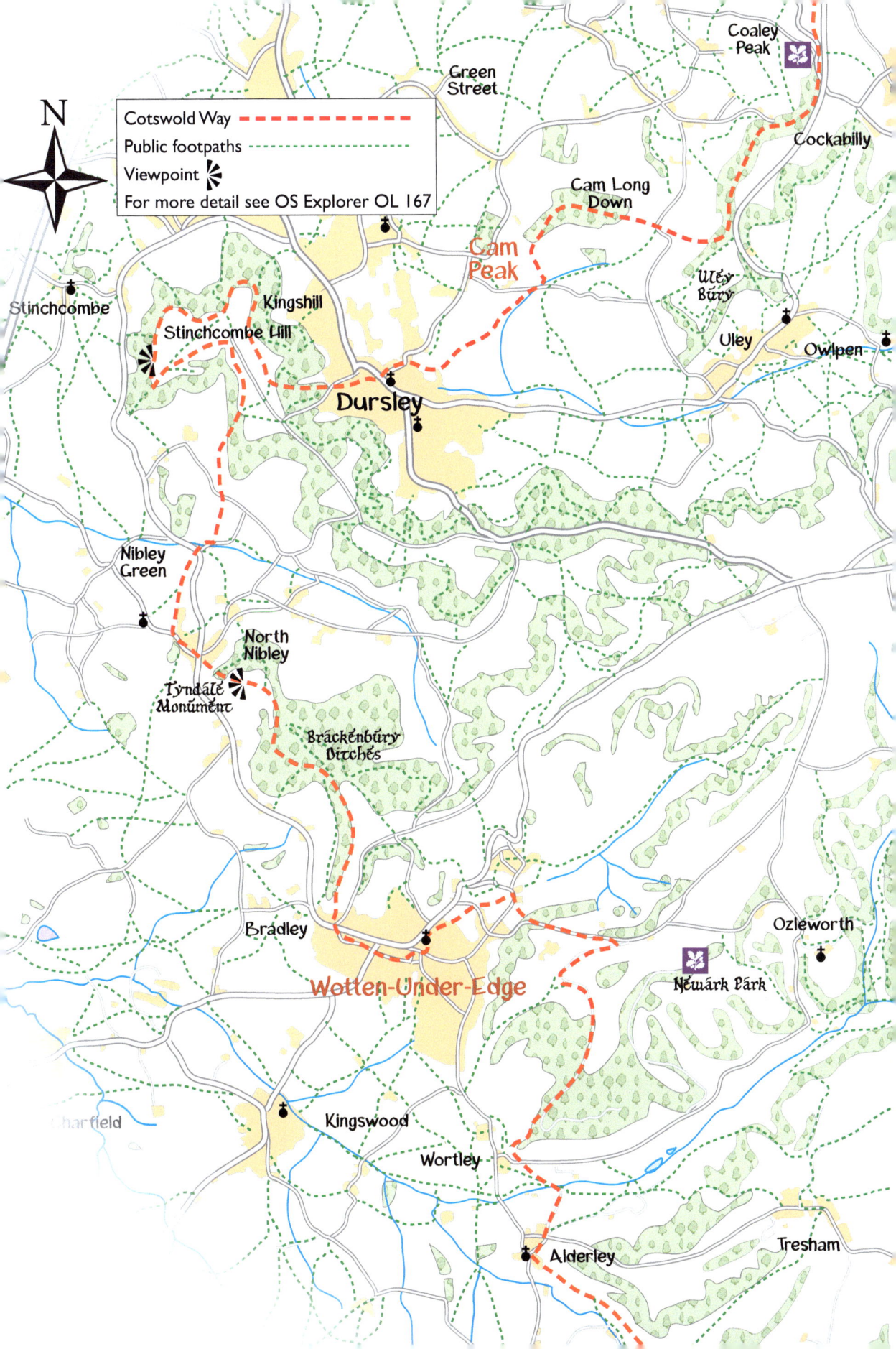

For more detail see OS Explorer OL 167

N

Cotswold Way
Public footpaths
Viewpoint

Coaley Peak

Cockabilly

Cam Long Down

Green Street

Cam Peak

Uley Bury

Kingshill

Uley

Stinchcombe

Stinchcombe Hill

Owlpen

Dursley

Nibley Green

North Nibley

Tyndale Monument

Brackenbury Ditches

Bradley

Ozleworth

Newark Park

Wotten-Under-Edge

Charfield

Kingswood

Wortley

Alderley

Tresham

on the final north eastern side by an additional berm with a concentric second outer rampart bank standing up to 7.6m wide and 1.5m high and an outer ditch of 6m wide and 1.2m deep with slightly offset entrances. It is thought this outer defensive line may represent a slightly later development phase of the hillfort. In the past internal natural hollows were misidentified as hut circles.

What you see today is the result of a lot of hard clearing work carried out by the South District Cotswold Voluntary Wardens.

The Tyndale Monument

Not long after the ditches, the trail passes the foot of the Tyndale Monument before descending the hill into North Nibley. The Tyndale Monument, commonly called 'Nibley Monument' locally, was built in honour of William Tyndale, the first translator of the New Testament into English, who was born nearby. As its Wikipedia entry explains, a Grade II listed building, the tower was constructed in 1866 and is 111 ft (34 metres) tall with features in common with the Somerset Monument built twenty years earlier. It is possible to enter and climb to the top of the tower, but it involves a spiral staircase of 121 steps! The hill it is on allows a wide range of views, especially looking down to the River Severn. A nearby topograph points to some other landmarks visible. The hill on which the monument stands is also quite steep. The path follows a rough fairly steep bridleway which is part of the Cotswold Way. The tower itself is surrounded by fencing and has flood lights that light up the tower at night. The stairway has automatic lighting. Locally, the hill is called Nibley Knoll or occasionally Nibley Knob rather than its official name. There is a commemorative plaque on the front of the tower. The text engraved on it reads:

ERECTED A.D. 1866 IN GRATEFUL REMEMBRANCE OF WILLIAM TYNDALE TRANSLATOR OF THE ENGLISH BIBLE WHO FIRST CAUSED THE NEW TESTAMENT TO BE PRINTED IN THE MOTHER TONGUE OF HIS COUNTRYMEN BORN NEAR THIS SPOT HE SUFFERED MARTYRDOM AT VILVORDEN IN FLANDERS ON OCT 6 1536

Inside the tower a narrow, dark, winding staircase leads to an enclosed viewing platform. If you have the energy and don't suffer from claustrophobia, the view is worth the climb. The monument is generally open to the public. If locked, see the notice board for where to get the key in North Nibley.

The monument is a landmark that can be seen for miles, even in places as far as Bristol over 20 miles away. In the town of Thornbury, there is a street called Tyndale View where the tower can be seen from approximately 10 miles (16 Kms) away. Its iconic position also helps to explain why, in October 2019, protesters from the Extinction Rebellion used the monument to display a protest banner.

The Wikipedia entry reminds us that Tyndale's translation was 'the first English Bible to draw directly from Hebrew and Greek texts, the first English translation to take advantage of the printing press, the first of the new English Bibles of the Reformation, and the first English translation to use Jehovah ('Iehouah') as God's name as preferred by English Protestant Reformers'. It was taken to be a direct challenge to the hegemony of both the Catholic Church and the laws of England maintaining the church's position.

Tyndale the man was pretty remarkable and deserves the attention he gets. He was born around 1494 at Melksham Court in nearby Stinchcombe, the family having moved to Gloucestershire from Northumberland at some point in the 15th century. He studied at both Oxford and Cambridge and,

The Tyndale Monument

over the years, became a gifted linguist. Apparently, he became fluent in French, Greek, Hebrew, German, Italian, Latin, and Spanish! As already noted, Tyndale became chaplain at the home of Sir John Walsh at Little Sodbury and tutor to his children around 1521.

Tyndale's opinions proved controversial to fellow clergymen on many issues and there were several dressing downs by the church authorities including one by the Chancellor of the Diocese of Worcester in 1525. Anxious to pursue his ambition to translate the New Testament, Tyndale left England for continental Europe, first possibly going to Hamburg and then travelling on to Wittenberg. It's here that he began translating the New Testament in earnest. A full edition was produced in 1526 in Worms and smuggled into England and Scotland. The church authorities responded by issuing warnings to booksellers and having copies burned in public.

Tyndale didn't always do himself any favours. In 1530, he opposed Henry VIII's planned annulment of his marriage to Catherine of Aragon in favour of Anne Boleyn. Not only was it unscriptural, he said, but part of a plot on the part of Cardinal Wolsey to get Henry entangled in the papal courts of Pope Clement VII. The king thereupon asked Emperor Charles V to have Tyndale apprehended and returned to England. Tyndale, it seems, managed to escape the clutches of his catholic pursuers for several years. Eventually, however, his luck ran out, when he was betrayed to authorities representing the Holy Roman Empire. He was seized in Antwerp in 1535 and held in the castle of Vilvoorde (Filford) near Brussels. Tried on a charge of heresy in 1536, he was found guilty and condemned to be burned to death, despite Thomas Cromwell's intercession on his behalf. In the event, Tyndale suffered the terrible fate of being 'strangled to death while tied at the stake, and then his dead body was burned'. His final words, spoken 'at the stake with a fervent zeal, and a loud voice', were reported as 'Lord! Open the King of England's eyes'. Whether Henry heard or not, four English translations of the Bible were published in England at the king's behest in as many years, including Henry's official Great Bible. All were based on Tyndale's work.

The Battle of Nibley Green

After the Tyndale Monument, the trail goes down to North Nibley. As well as being noted for its Black Horse Inn - and a slightly dangerous road crossing - Nibley also has a couple of other properties of interest. Nibley House, next to the church, was the home of John Smyth, steward of Berkeley Castle and the estates of the Berkeley family, and author of *Lives of the Berkeleys*. He was also involved through the Virginia Company in the early settlement of that state.

Close by, too, is Swinway House which the McMurtry family from Wotton-under-Edge commissioned. Apparently, the client's vision was to create a futuristic house that provides for an active lifestyle both inside and out. The result was a ten-level, eight-bedroom country home of 33,000 square feet (3,100 square metres) on a 60-acre site. The conceptual design, developed with David Austin, is said to respect 'the property's Cotswold location and delivers the client's distinctive and modern vision through the use of traditional Cotswold stone, alongside glass, steel and wood'.

It seems that the McMurties don't live in the house. Instead it is used to host charitable causes and rented out to fashion photographers and filmmakers. In 2014 the final episode of the third series of BBC One's *Sherlock* featured Swinhay House.

Also close by, Nibley Green is said to have been the site of the last battle in Britain between private armies. To quote Wikipedia:

> The Battle of Nibley Green was fought near North Nibley in Gloucestershire on 20 March 1470, between the troops of Thomas Talbot, 2nd Viscount Lisle and William Berkeley, 2nd Baron Berkeley. Lisle and Berkeley had long been engaged in a dispute over the inheritance of Berkeley Castle and the other Berkeley lands, Lisle being heir-general to Thomas de Berkeley, 5th Baron Berkeley and Berkeley heir-male. Lisle impetuously challenged Berkeley to a battle, and the latter agreed, the battle to be fought the next day at Nibley Green. Lisle paid for his rashness with his life.

Stinchcombe Hill - thank you Sir Stanley

On your way to Stinchcombe Hill, you have Stancombe Park and its Temple on the left. Stancombe Park, where there was a house of some substance with a small park and lake, was part of the estate of the Purnell family of Dursley. It remains in private hands, but its Grade One listed ashlar Doric Temple in the Folly Gardens is available to rent if you'd like a romantic break in the Cotswolds.

The temple and gardens are said to have been the inspiration of the reverend David Purnell-Edwards towards the end of the 19th century. The story goes, according to the website devoted to The Temple, that he married a 'portly' lady and, aided by her large dowry, embarked on the idea of an idealised walk which would encapsulate all the important civilisations around the two acre lake: it's made up of Chinese, Egyptian and Greek architectural styles. Apparently, though, the tunnels were scarcely enough for the wife to fit through.

Coming onto Stinchcombe Hill, you have a choice of routes to Dursley. There's a direct route via the golf club house on your right or a circuit of the hill, which adds a couple of miles.

Stinchcombe Hill itself is noted for superb views from the Cotswold Way above steep slopes in all directions and supporting a wide biodiversity of flora and wildlife. Large areas of the summit

The view from Drakestone Point on Stinchcombe Hill

and hillsides including three SSSIs support important areas of 'unimproved' Cotswold limestone grassland.

More problematic is the archaeological status of what is known as 'Drakestone Point'. It consists of natural ridges and gullies cutting off a very small part of the narrow tapering tip of the ridge. It's a promontory that's revealed many ancient features with relics of a long military history found nearby. As Gloucestershire County Council's *Heritage Gateway* explains, it's been variously described as an Iron Age hillfort camp, a signal station and a motte and castle. The jury remains out. It seems, though, that some of the features are natural rather than man made. On the evidence at present available, it seems, the so-called hill-fort of Drakestone point cannot be regarded as an historic monument.

Stinchcombe Hill is also special on account of its ownership. The land comprising the top of Stinchcombe Hill, commonly called 'The Hill', was originally owned by three families or estates. The greater part belonged to the Berkeley Estate, the next largest part belonged to the Stancombe Estate, being owned by the Purnell family, and the remainder formed part of the Stinchcombe Estate owned by the Prevost family. In 1929, however, its more than 200 acres was registered with the Charity Commissioners and administered by The Stinchcombe Hill Recreation Ground Trust to promote 'public access for walking and horse-riding plus a full access condition for the Hill Parishes in partnership with the Historic Stinchcombe Hill Golf Course'. A joint intensive programme by local conservation volunteers and the Golf Club to restore viewpoints and hillsides to grassland from scrub and tree incursion has enabled the new Cotswold Trail to fully circle the hill and pass through two lost glades.

The Trust tells what it calls 'the story of the hill' like this:

Originally Stinchcombe Hill had been sheep-grazed in various ownerships but this started to change in 1889 with the formation of Stinchcombe Hill Golf Club, first with a nine hole course and later with a full 18 holes. At that time the Club rented the land, but in the 1920s there was a threat of housing being built over the hill.

Fortunately this never materialised thanks to the generosity of businessman Sir Stanley Tubbs, of Wotton-under-Edge, whose family owned the prosperous Tubbs, Lewis and Co at Kingswood.

Sir Stanley, who was a former president of Stinchcombe Hill Golf Club, persuaded the owners to sell him the land in order to secure the long-term future of the Hill and the golf club. He completed the purchases at a cost of £1,217 in 1928, and on January 6, 1929, granted a 99 year lease to the golf club at an annual rental of £20; shortly afterwards setting up the charity known as the Stinchcombe Hill Recreation Ground Trust, to administer the hill.

The area covered not only includes the 135 acres of golf course, but a further 50 acres of woodlands given to the then Dursley Rural District Council, and also the Drakestone area, together with grassland tracts outside the course.

In giving the club their lease Sir Stanley was mindful of the needs of the local population (residents of the parishes of Dursley, Cam, Stinchcombe and North Nibley and neighbourhood), and specified that, while the priority on the course lay with the golfers, save on the public footpaths, bridleways, and permissive rides, local residents had "the right to use the lands for air and recreation, but only at such times and in such manner as shall not impede or interfere with the use thereof as a golf course".

It is believed that Sir Stanley Tubbs' Benefaction was, at the date when it was established, the largest single one of its type within the County of Gloucester.

Dursley and the Listers

The trail descends into Dursley, which is the largest town on the Cotswold Way. It gets you through very quickly via May Street and Parsonage Street and then a left via the Market House and St James the Great into Long Street.

Architecturally, it has to be said, Dursley doesn't really stand comparison with most of the other towns on the trail, being at the junction of three main streets creating a market area. Many of these buildings date back to the 18th and early 19th centuries. The major feature is the Market House. Dating from 1738, when the town's markets attracted farmers and traders from miles around, it's noted for its pillared build, bell turret and statue of Queen Anne.

The earliest reference to a church building here is in 1221 when it was a sanctuary church. About 1320, the church was enlarged and rebuilt using 'puff' stone as seen in the two arcades of octagonal columns. A tower with a spire was built in 1480, new roof put on and the fine perpendicular windows put in. It was a time of great prosperity because of the local woollen trade. However, the spire and tower fell down in 1698 and the tower alone was rebuilt as it's now seen in 1707 - 1709.

Perhaps the major consideration in Dursley's development compared to that of Wotton is that it achieved market and borough status much later. Critically, it doesn't seem to have a major market for buying wool. Its rise to prominence was in the 1500s, when it became one of the principal cloth making centres along the scarp. Long Lane, which leads you out of Dursley, is where there were several medieval mills.

Dursley Glos Web, which is the website of the Dursley & Cam Society, is a fund of information about the town's industrial past. By the 16th century the wool trade, it points out, was established in the Ewelme (or Cam) valley and the area became famous for its fine 'broadcloths'. It wasn't just this cloth, though, that the area was known for; there were many others - twill, cassimere, buckskin, medley, serge and worsted were all produced in the local mills.

Cloth making in the area began as a cottage industry with individuals often working out of their own homes, perhaps working for many masters and walking miles to collect and return materials. By the late eighteenth century, the clothiers realised that it was to their advantage to get all their workers together under one roof and this led to the rise of the factory system.

Boom years followed. In 1820 there were eight cloth mills operating in Dursley. The bubble quickly burst, however. By 1840 there were five and by 1860 they had all closed. In that year the only mill still operational in the locality was the one at Cam Mill, which was still open in 2009. New machines, powered by steam as well as water, caused a surplus of labour and overproduction led to wage cuts. Mills began to close and clothiers left the industry fearful of losing their wealth in the downturn. There were riots and strikes. Indeed, in 1827 troops were sent into Dursley to quell any uprising.

Heavy engineering might be said to have come to Dursley's rescue and for what it became best known for. The 1860s saw the establishment of R. A. Lister and Company which went on to become the town's largest employer with upwards of 4000 employees at its peak. Initially, card-making and wire-drawing were the main products. Very quickly, however, these were followed by a wide range of agricultural machinery, notably sheep shearing machinery, milking machines and milk churn and barrel making. The 'Alexandra Cream Separator', the invention of the Danish inventor Mikael Pedersen, was launched in 1878 to much acclaim. Pedersen himself moved to Dursley shortly afterwards to work in the dairy section of R.A. Lister before going on to set up the Dursley Pedersen Cycle Company, more of which below.

Moving on to the 20th century, engine production came to dominate. Initially, Listers were associated with petrol engines. It was the coming of the diesel engine, however, which was to play a huge part in the company's fortunes. By 1936, Lister's is said to have been the largest manufacturer of diesel engines of their kind in the world and produced a range of 80 different sizes and types of diesel and petrol models. They were also making very large quantities of pumps, churns, cream separators, autotrucks, generating plant and sheep shearing equipment.

Production continued apace through the late 1940s, 1950s and 1960s with constant introduction of new engines, predominantly diesels. Between the years of 1951 and 1969, 56 different new models entered the company's portfolio and another 19 were withdrawn. In 1948, much reorganisation of the factory took place and modern machines and production facilities were introduced.

Sadly, the company found it difficult to hold its own in the increasingly competitive market place in recent decades. It was only in 2014 that production finally ended: assembly production moved to Hardwicke and the parts supply store to a former Royal Air Force hangar at Aston Down. Lister Petter, was based in the town until 2014, though much of the original 92-acre (37 ha) factory site was acquired in 2000 by the South West Regional Development Agency and then in 2011 by Stroud District Council. It is now being developed as a large housing development with some industrial units.

Production may have ceased, but the Lister name nonetheless lives on in Dursley. The 'Tower', a large gothic-style house and formerly part of the Lister Petter estate, still overlooks the town and has been converted into flats and a residential care home. Dursley's theatre, Lister Hall, also bears the company name - the building was formerly part of the social centre for the firm. Many of Listers' engines, it is also reckoned, are still likely to be in use today all over the world.

Closely associated with Listers' is the Danish inventor Mikael Pedersen. He came to Dursley in 1897 at the invitation of the Listers to set up local assembly of his acclaimed machine for churning and separating cream and butter from milk. Later, Pedersen started up manufacture of his unusual and ingenious cantilevered bicycle, which went on to earn a small, but devoted following.

Unfortunately, Pedersen doesn't seem to have been as good a businessman as an inventor. He left Dursley unannounced in his sixties and returned to Denmark, where he died in poverty in 1927 followed by burial in an unmarked grave in a Copenhagen suburb. There was something of a happy ending, though. In 1995 Pedersen bicycle enthusiasts raised the money to bring his remains back to Dursley for re-burial there. The service, it's reported, was attended by over 300 people including the Bishop of Gloucester, Danish Embassy representatives and Pedersen's grandchildren.

So why, going back to Chapter 1, did J.K. Rowling, author of the Harry Potter books and born in nearby Yate, name the unlikable Dursley family after the town? Some say it's because she didn't like Dursley. Rowling herself is reported on *Harry Potter Wiki* to have written on her digital publishing Pottermore website:

> *The surname 'Dursley' was taken from the eponymous town in Gloucestershire, which is not very far from where I was born. I have never visited Dursley, and I expect that it is full of charming people. It was the sound of the word that appealed, rather than any association with the place.*

In a 2001 interview she did add: 'I don't imagine I'm very popular in Dursley'. Just for the record, Dursley first appeared in public records in 1086 as Dersilege, which simply means 'woodland clearing of a man called Deorsige'.

Up to Cam Peak

Leaving Dursley, you pass the Bowls Club on your left and Downham Hill on your right. The latter is known locally as 'Smallpox Hill' because in the 17th century it was the site of an isolation facility for victims of the disease.

Cam Peak, sometimes known as 'Peaked Down', is your final destination on this stage. The unusual conical shape of Cam Peak is visible close to the north of the town and appears almost artificial in nature, although it is in fact entirely natural in origin. It's by no means the highest hill in the Cotswolds reaching just 722 ft (220 metres). But it is a short steep climb to the top and an interpretation panel. Adjacent to the elongated shape of Cam Long Down, which features in the next Chapter, there are wonderful views across to Dursley, Cam, the Vale of Berkeley, Coaley, Uley Valley and beyond to the escarpment near Nympsfield and across the Severn to the Forest of Dean.

Cotswold Way Circular Walk

Cam Long Down and Uley are the location of one of the twelve Cotswold Way Circular Walks. It's No 9. In the words of the National Trails website:

'The incredible variety of the Cotswold Way is once again explored by this stunning little walk. From woodland tracks to open hilltops, it leads you around the intriguing ancient history of Uley Bury to the more recent remains of a pestilent past. Even the few hillside climbs are rewarded by compass-wide views that spread out all around you back into the heart of the Cotswolds and across the Severn Estuary into Wales…'

- Distance: 4 miles (shorter route: 1½ miles. Duration: 2½ – 3½ hours (shorter: ¾ – 1½ hours). Difficulty: Moderate to difficult – Some stiles, steps and steep sections'.
- You can download the map from www.nationaltrail.co.uk

Cotswold Way Friendship Walk

Stinchcombe Hill is the location of one of the two friendship walks on the Cotswold Way. It's entitled 'The Cotswolds Korea Friendship Trail'. In the words of the National Trails website:

'The Cotswold Way has teamed up with South Korea's Jeju Olle Trail to become one of the world's first 'friendship trails'. Follow this short walk around Stinchcombe Hill to experience one of the most beautiful meanderings of the Cotswold Way and discover a new world of walking on an island five thousand miles away.'

- Distance: 3½ miles (hill only route: 3 miles). Duration: 2 – 2½ hours (hill only: 1 ½ – 2 hours). Difficulty: Moderate – firm surface, no stiles, one long steep ascent / descent (Hill only: Easy – firm surface, no stiles, mostly level)'.
- You can download the map from www.nationaltrail.co.uk

NB You might like to know that there's also a 1.5 (2kms) Miles without stiles variant. You can download this walk as well.

Car Parking

- For the start in Wotton-Under-Edge, see the end point on the previous stage.
- At Cam Peak, there's a car park shown on the OS map on the hill itself (approximate postcode GL11 5HD). An alternative in Dursley is the May Lane car park (GL11 4JQ).
- If you'd like to tackle the Circular Walk No 9, you're advised to park in Uley (GL11 5SN). You'll find a couple of suggested parking places on the downloadable map.

Chapter 7
Barrows, hills and mills
Cam Peak to Haresfield

The bulk of the walking on this stage takes place in glorious woodland. Even so, of all the stages, this is perhaps the most varied. At the beginning, you'll be walking on one of the escarpment outliers, where you will find perhaps the most impressive of all the Cotswold hill forts, two long barrows and a temple. Later on, the trail offers you a choice of routes enabling you to bypass the most built-up area on the Cotswold Way. If you take the opportunity, you'll cross a common and walk along a canal towpath with mill buildings that remind us how important cloth making once was. There's a recently established vineyard, too, recalling the listing of two such enterprises in the 1086's Domesday Book. After more earthworks, the stage ends with several miles of more fine woodland walking that takes you to the top of a hill with a famous beacon.

Cam Long Down to Nympsfield - hidden gems aplenty

From Cam Peak, which is the start of this stage, Cam Long Down is just a few metres further on. It's higher, but not by much. It's a wonderful ridge walk with great views all round - for many it ranks in the top half dozen of the Cotswolds as a whole. The pity is that it's over too quickly. There are signs of earthworks and ancient pit dwellings on the down, but they are very slight. Large quantities of worked flints have also been found.

Just off to the right after Springfield farm and on the scarp-edge is Uley Bury - an impressive multi-vallate Iron Age hill fort dating from around 300 BCE. In the words of Historic England:

> *The monument includes a large multivallate hillfort situated on and occupying the entire summit of a distinctive and steeply sloping Cotswold plateau which forms the watershed between the valleys of the River Ewelme and one of its major tributaries. The hillfort survives as a roughly rectangular enclosure covering approximately 23ha which is defined by double terraces and augmented steep scarp slopes with slight banks above and which has a main entrance to the north and smaller ones to the east and south. In 1976 excavation works prior to the laying of pipelines produced a crouched burial, indicated one of the entrances was turf and timber lined with a metalled road and produced Iron Age pottery, shale armlets, a glass bead, a bronze ring headed pin and two Iron Age currency bars. Further evidence in the form of well over 2000 flint artefacts indicates the presence of a pre Iron Age settlement on the summit, probably of Neolithic origin.*

Green
Street

Cam
Peak

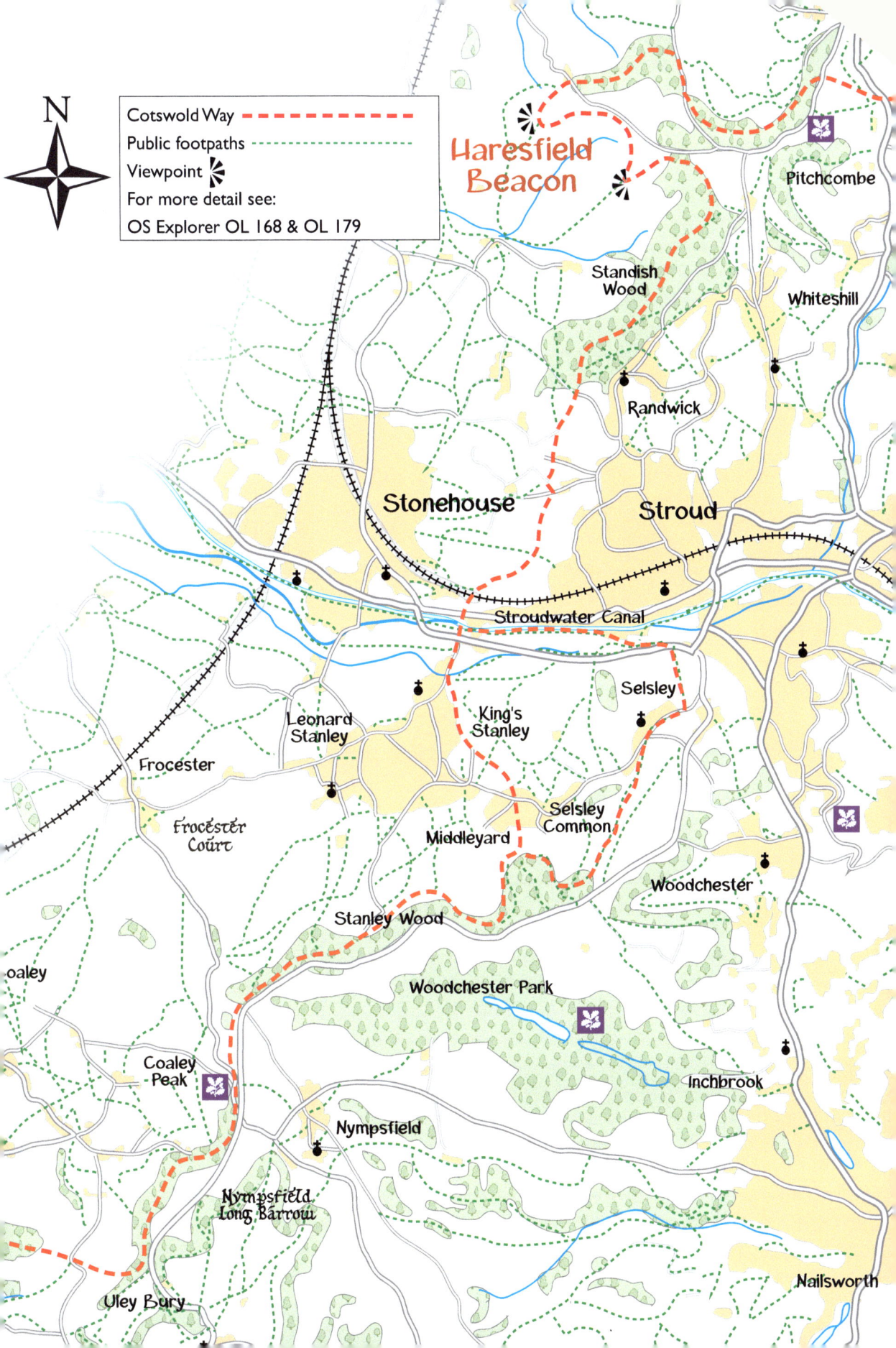

N

Haresfield
Beacon

Pitchcombe

Standish
Wood

Whiteshill

Randwick

Stonehouse

Stroud

Stroudwater Canal

Selsley

Leonard
Stanley

King's
Stanley

Frocester

Frocester
Court

Selsley
Common

Middleyard

Woodchester

Stanley Wood

Woodchester Park

oaley

Coaley
Peak

Inchbrook

Nympsfield

Nympsfield
Long Barrow

Nailsworth

Uley Bury

The footpath around Uley Bury

Uley Bury is reckoned to be one of the largest and most impressive of all the Cotswold hill forts with evidence of occupation from approximately 300 BCE to 100 AD. The Bury is surrounded on all sides, apart from at the northern corner, by steep natural slopes. The hill fort was created by terracing a double line of ramparts – more than a mile (1.6 Kms) in length overall - into the hillsides. Excavations carried out on the north eastern rampart during the 1970s found evidence of how the ramparts were constructed. Aerial photography has revealed extensive crop marks, suggesting that there were once numerous dwellings in the interior of the hill fort; however, these have not yet been excavated.

Shortly after on your right, on West Hill, are the remains of a late Iron Age shrine that became a Romano-British Temple. Extensive excavation in the late 1970s suggested several stages. In the earliest, probably the 4th millennium BCE, it comprised standing stones or posts at the focus of an open ended enclosure. In around 200 AD the wooden shrine was replaced by stone square structure similar to other Romano-Celtic temples In the 2nd or 1st century BCE a sequence of ditched and palisaded enclosures were built around two shrines of timber construction that may have stood within a sacred woodland clearance. The central shrine was replaced on the same axis in the early 2nd century AD by a stone Romano Celtic temple dedicated to a cult of Mercury. Ranged around about were buildings in timber and stone, living quarters for the priests and accommodation for visitors. As well as fragments of a limestone statue of Mercury, finds included numerous lead tablets, many inscribed with curses, and animal bones, indicating the sacrificial remains of goat, sheep, and cockerels. Following modifications in the 4th century AD, the temple was levelled in the 5th century, and in its place a timber hall or basilican church was constructed on the earlier axis; this building was later reconstructed in stone and was used as a Christian place of worship down to the 7th or 8th centuries AD.

Next up, not visible from the route, but accessible from the road above, is Uley Long Barrow - known also as 'Hetty Peglers Tump' after the wife of the 17th century owner of the site. Although typically described as a long barrow, the proper technical term for the mound is said to be a 'transepted gallery grave'. It was probably built before 3000 BCE. It measures about 37 metres (121 ft) long, 34 metres (112 ft) wide, and has a maximum height of 3 metres (9.8 ft). It contains a stone-built central passage with two chambers on either side and another at the end. The earthen mound is surrounded by a dry-stone revetting wall. The barrow was archaeologically excavated in 1821, revealing the remains of fifteen skeletons and a later, intrusive Roman age burial above the northeast chamber. It was excavated again in 1854. In the words of Historic England:

The barrow has a mound composed of small stones; it is trapezoidal in plan and orientated from north-east to south-west. It has dimensions of 51m by 30m and stands to a maximum height of 3m. At the eastern end of the monument there is a forecourt consisting of a recess flanked on either side by projections of mound. This forecourt has dimensions of 12.5m by 2.5m and leads into a north-east facing entrance defined by two standing stones capped by a stone lintel. Beyond the entrance is a stone gallery 1m wide and 10m long, which leads into two pairs of side chambers and an end chamber. These chambers have average dimensions of 1m in width, 3m in depth and 1.2m in height.

The excavations of 1821 revealed that there were skeletons and the lower jaws of several wild boar. Four skeletons were recovered from the eastern side chamber, including one of a woman, along with finds of animal teeth and Neolithic pottery, accompanied by three Roman coins dating to the Constantinian period (AD 312-337). This, it is said, represents an intrusive Romano-British burial.

Believe it or not, but in less than a mile north there is yet another barrow - Nympsfield Long Barrow. Historic England describes it like this:

The monument ... has a mound which is almost oval in plan, with dimensions of 30m from east to west, 25m from north to south at the western end and 30m from north to south at the eastern end. The mound is composed of small stones and has a maximum height of c.1.1m. At the eastern end of the mound is a forecourt in the form of a recess flanked by projections of the mound. This forecourt has dimensions of 4m by 4.5m and leads into an east facing entrance defined by two standing stones. Beyond the entrance is a stone gallery, now unroofed, and which leads into a pair of side chambers and an end chamber. The remains of at least 13 human skeletons as well as Neolithic pottery were recovered from these chambers, the associated gallery and from the surrounding mound during excavations ... in 1862 and ... in 1937. These excavations also found later Neolithic pottery within the blocking of the entrance to the burial chamber, suggesting that the gallery was closed before the end of the Neolithic period. The mound is flanked on each side by a quarry ditch from which material was taken during the construction of the monument. These ditches have become infilled over the years, but survive as buried features c.3m wide.

Historic England adds that Nympsfield Long Barrow is a good example of the group of long barrows commonly referred to as the 'Cotswold Severn group', mentioned in Chapter 2 and named after the region in which they occur. Belas Knap above Winchcombe, which you'll come across in Chapter 11, is perhaps the best known example. Nympsfield is one of very few oval long barrows which belong to the group.

Retrace a few steps from Nympsfield barrow and return to Coaley Peak, which offers 12 acres (4.9 ha) of reclaimed farmland (now a wild flower meadow) with views over the Severn Vale and the Forest of Dean. It's next to a Woodland Trust beech wood and the National Trust's Frocester Hill site. If you like, from Coaley Peak, you can make a short detour to Frocester Hill, which is just a 5-minute walk to the south of Coaley Peak, and is indicated by a stone marker. From Frocester Hill, you can enjoy further glorious views reaching out for miles.

Frocester Court

Close by is the village of Frocester and its Grade II listed building of Frocester Court. Once much larger, it was vastly reduced in size in the mid 19th century. Parts of the house, however, predate the Reformation, with some dating from the 15th century. The name of the village, first recorded in the Domesday Book as 'Frowecestre', means 'Roman town on the Frome'. Frocester was the site of a Roman settlement on the road which ran from Cirencester to Arlingham. The remains of a Roman villa have been excavated in the grounds of Frocester Court.

Into Stanley country

After Nympsfield Long Barrow, the trail continues through Buckholt Wood followed by Stanley Wood. It's the first 'Stanley' of many: Kings Stanley, Leonard Stanley and later Stanley Mill. Even Selsley, it seems, was unable to escape the influence, much of it being called 'Stanley End' until recently, as well as hosting Stanley Park.

It's not altogether clear why the name is so prolific. At first sight, the answer is fairly simple. Britain was once covered in dense woodland and forest. There were, however, stony places where no trees could grow and this was where early inhabitants built their settlements. These areas were known as 'stanleys' or 'stony ground', being derived from 'stan' (pebble/stone) and 'leah' (clearing). A number of other words meaning rocky, also give their names to local places including Stantone - the former name of the neighbouring village of King's Stanley and Standish. Unfortunately, there is a little confusion as to the original name, because the Domesday Book entry for the village refers to it as Stanlege. Never mind, says the local Council, it was a good theory!

Anyway, as you progress through the several miles of Stanley Wood, look out for gliders. This because over to your right is the airstrip of the Bristol and Gloucestershire Gliding Club running for over a kilometre along the top of the Cotswold escarpment. Also to the right, and sharing a common boundary, is the National Trust's Woodchester Park estate to which there is footpath access from the Cotswold Way.

When you come to Pen Hill and the Wood of the same name, you have two possibilities - one goes up through Middleyard and past Kings Stanley. The other, the 'scenic' route, goes right to Selsley.

Beech trees in Stanley Wood

You're strongly advised to take the scenic route. Don't forget the Stanleys altogether, though, because they were formerly one of the most populous of the Stroudwater clothing parishes, with a strong Flemish presence. An early King's Stanley parish register records in the frontispiece that 'There was a large immigration of Flemish families to the neighbourhood in the time of Edward III in the mid-1300s for the weaving and making of cloth of the wool of the upland country'. In 1608, 81 people were employed in cloth, 18 in other trades and 27 in agriculture. By 1633, 800 persons in King's and neighbouring Leonard Stanley were dependent upon the cloth industry. Until well into the 19th century, weaving was still done on hand looms situated in the workers' cottages. The 1851 census for King's Stanley records large numbers of hand loom workers living in the village and it's said that even in 1863 it was possible to hear the click of the loom shuttle from the cottages as people rode through the village. You might also like to know that the great-grandfather of Wild West outlaw Jesse James reportedly came from Kings Stanley.

On the short route, just beyond Kings Stanley and before Ryeford, is Stanley Mill with a mill pond on its right: the main building has been turned into flats with new houses built on the adjacent lands. There had been mills on the site for many years, but the current mill was built in 1813 and expanded around 1825. Claimed to be the largest in Gloucestershire, its weaving looms were powered by five water wheels on the River Frome and the workforce numbered some 1000 people in its early years. The mill added steam power in 1827 and continued production until the 1980's, being owned by the Marling family for many of the intervening years.

Looking at the map, you might wonder why there has been no mention of Middleyard. Basically, it's because it seems to have little or no history. Indeed, the name 'Middle Yard' was apparently used only for a single house in 1749. Most of the houses date from the late 18th and early 19th centuries. A mid

20th century housing estate to the south-west of Middle Yard around Pen Lane completes the picture.

Selsley Common and the Stroudwater Canal

As for the 'scenic' route, after Pen Wood, the trail crosses Selsley Common for a couple of miles. The Common is an open plateau 200 metres or so above sea level. In the words of the *Trailblazer Guide*, it offers 'exhilarating walking' with 'plenty of places to sit and gaze'. If you don't know the common well, you're strongly advised to keep to the Cotswold Way waymarks. Otherwise, the wild grass and undulating landscape may be disorienting.

The Wikipedia entry tells us that attempts to enclose the Common have been vigorously resisted down through the centuries - the first recorded dispute was in Anglo-Saxon times. There is one area which did become enclosed, though, known locally as 'Dead Man's Acre'. The story goes that a man was told that he could have as much land of the common that he could enclose in one day. Sadly, the effort proved too much and killed him. The truth of this tale is dubious, critics say, because it bears too many similarities to works of fiction such as Leo Tolstoy's *How Much Land Does a Man Need?*

The church of All Saints that you come to on the left at the end of the Common is Victorian. It's particularly notable in the development of the arts and crafts movement touched on in Chapter 2. Its stained glass windows were one of the first commissions for Willam Morris' design company.

In the mid 1800s, Selsley itself was divided into Selsley West and Selsley. Previously Selsley West was a series of hamlets known as Stanley End, Picked (or Peaked) Elm and The Knapp, with The Knapp east of present day Middleyard, Stanley End closer to the modern Selsley village, and Picked Elm the houses near Peaked Elm Farm.

Stanley Park is the original manor house in Selsley West dating from the time of Elizabeth I. The house was rebuilt in the mid-18th century and then further remodelled when it was bought by the Marling family in 1850. The house and estate was sold in 1952, with the house divided into flats.

Stanley Park was the destination of pioneering Oxford balloonist, James Sadler, on the first ever flight from Stroud on 19 October 1785. It was estimated that the flight was watched by 40,000 people.

After Selsley, the trail drops down to the Stroudwater Canal, which is 8 miles (12.8 kms) in length rising 102 feet through 12 locks. It was built between 1775 and 1779 from Framilode, on the banks of the River Severn, to Wallbridge (Stroud) to service the woollen mills. Early success led the Stroudwater Canal Company to seek to extend its reach towards London, which it did in 1789 via the Sapperton Tunnel. Competition from the railways in the late 19th century, however, meant the canal was never a great success owing to the loss of water in the porous Cotswold stone. It was eventually closed in 1941. It's now managed by the Cotswold Canals Trust and, as with all such canals, its overriding purpose is one of amenity and leisure.

Just after the trail passes left in reaching Dudbridge, you will pass Ebley Mill on the banks of the River Frome. Ebley Mill was built in 1820 and operated until 1981. In the 1800s, it was one of the largest woollen cloth mills in the Stroud area, employing 800 people in the 1870s. The building is Grade II listed and now used as the offices of Stroud District Council.

Between Stonehouse and Stroud

The Stroudwater Canal

At Ryeford, the trail runs between Stonehouse to your left and Stroud to the right. Stonehouse appears in the Domesday Book of 1086 under its Old English name 'Stanhus' – so called, it is believed, because the manor house was built of stone rather than the usual wattle and daub. The woollen industry was important to Stonehouse people, first as producers of wool and later as experts in textiles. The small mills of the 17th and 18th century supported work at home for the growing population of the village, later changing to a factory system.

As for Stroud, the small rivers which flow through its five valleys made it into an ideal position for the production of cloth. Altogether it is estimated there might have been at one time as many as 150 mills crowding these valleys. Known as the 'string of pearls', the line of mills was internationally famous for its broadcloth. Indeed, it was widely known as 'Stroud cloth'. Particularly noteworthy was the production of military uniforms in the colour 'Stroudwater Scarlet'. Notable, too, is that the area became home to a sizable Huguenot community in the 17th century, fleeing persecution in Catholic France. At the end of the 19th century, a Jewish community also established itself as the demand for men's tailoring expanded.

As the trail heads northwards towards Westrip, it passes Doverow Hill. Here you will find the recently opened Woodchester Valley Vineyard with the vineyards under the hollowed out stone quarry at the top of the hill. Surprised? You shouldn't really be. In the Domesday book of 1086 two vineyards were recorded in Stonehouse!

Through Standish Wood - on the Robbers' Road

The final leg of this stage takes you for several miles through Standish Woods until you reach your destination, which is the Shortwood National Trust car park on Haresfield Hill. As well as being renowned for its mixed beech with lovely lime green foliage, Standish Wood has a wealth of archaeological features. Initially, the trail follows 'Robbers Road', sometimes known as 'Thieves Lane', passing Randwick Hill Long Barrow on the right. Historic England offers this description:

The monument, which falls into three separate areas of protection, includes a long barrow, two bowl barrows and a cross dyke situated on the summit of a prominent ridge which is part of the Cotswold Escarpment and forms the watershed between the valleys of the Ruscombe Brook and a tributary to the River Severn and overlooks the Vale of Gloucester. The long barrow survives as a roughly rectangular mound orientated ENE to WSW measuring up to 45.7m long, 26.2m wide and 4.5m high. The side ditches are preserved as entirely buried features. Excavated in 1883 it was found to have a 'horned' entrance and a chamber defined by drystone walls at the

Woodchester Valley Vineyard at Doverow Hill

eastern end. The chamber contained at least seven skeletons and above these a Roman horse shoe and Roman pottery were recovered. The barrow mound was found to be surrounded by a retaining drystone wall and several crouched inhumations were discovered beside this wall on the south side of the mound.

The bowl barrows survive as circular mounds of between 8m and 9m in diameter and from 0.6m up to 0.9m high surrounded by visible quarry ditches from which the construction material was derived. One has a slight central depression. The cross dyke is a linear earthwork bank and adjacent ditch measuring up to 200m long, the bank is up to 0.7m high and the ditch approximately 0.6m deep.

The first recording of the name 'Standish' is as early as the year 872 AD in the spelling of Stanedis, in Gloucestershire and in Lancashire. In both cases the meaning is the same, being the 'park enclosed by a stone wall', from the Olde English pre-7th century words 'stan', meaning stone, and 'edisc', an enclosed park.

Below the wood lies Standish Park, which was first listed in 1297 in connection with Gloucester Abbey. It is known that in 1515 it provided '12 cart-loads of beechwood a year for the lessee of the demesne to be delivered by the woodward'. Later in the century, the beechwood is reported to have been providing 20 cartloads. The park, it seems, was originally part of Standish Court originally built by Abbot of Gloucester in the 14th century in the nearby village of the same name. In 1612 the park apparently amounted to around 250 acres.

Standish Park was also for many years home to a 100+ bed hospital. Being unoccupied at the time, Lord Sherborne was persuaded to agree to Standish House being opened as a British Red Cross Hospital in 1915 not long after the beginning of WW1. After the war, Gloucestershire County Council bought the house in its entirety and turned it into a sanatorium to treat tuberculosis. In 1948, the hospital became part of the National Health Service and specialized in orthopaedics, rheumatology and respiratory care across the whole of Gloucestershire. It only closed in 2004, becoming recently available for redevelopment for residential use. Fortunately, in 1931, the National Trust had been able to acquire Standish Wood, along with Haresfield Beacon, to protect it from development.

When you reach the car park Shortwood (sometimes known as Cripplegate), the one thing you must do is go up to the topograph for the views. You can even go onto the Beacon if you have the energy. Don't feel you have to, though. The Beacon and the surrounding Haresfield area will be the starting point of the next chapter

---

Cotswold Way Circular Walks

This stage is the location of two of the twelve Cotswold Way Circular Walks. The first of these, No 9, is entitled **'Cam Long Down and Uley'**. In the words of the National Trails website:

'The incredible variety of the Cotswold Way is once again explored by this stunning little walk. From woodland tracks to open hilltops, it leads you around the intriguing ancient history of Uley Bury to the more recent remains of a pestilent past. Even the few hillside climbs are rewarded by compass-wide views that spread out all around you back into the heart of the Cotswolds and across the Severn Estuary into Wales.

- Distance: 4 miles (shorter route: 1½ miles). Duration: 2½ – 3½ hours (shorter: ¾ – 1½ hours). Difficulty: Moderate to difficult – Some stiles, steps and steep sections'.
- You can download the map from www.nationaltrail.co.uk

The second Circular Walk, No 8, is entitled **'The Selsley Circuit'**. In the words of the National Trails website:

'This extremely popular walk is one of the easiest to follow, winding its way along the National Trail for nearly all of its length. From sheltered beech woodlands and over rich open grassland, it guides you around remnants of an industrial past that shaped the landscape we love today. Wander between the grandeur of Victorian mills alongside the sleepy beauty of the waterway, and discover a timeless journey between past and present that reveals yet another face of the glorious Cotswolds.

- Distance: 5 miles. Duration: 3 – 4 hours. Difficulty: Moderate – Three stiles, some steep sections'.
- You can download the map from www.nationaltrail.co.uk

Cotswold Way Friendship Walk

This stage is also the location of the second of the Cotswold Way's friendship walks. It's entitled 'Bruce Friendship Trail – Beacons, Commons and Woods (Standish Wood, Harescombe Beacon and Pitchcombe Wood)'. In the words of the National Trails website:

'This spectacular walk leads you along peaceful woodland tracks and out onto windswept hillsides with breath-taking views. A true jewel in the Cotswolds crown. Not only is it a stunning route, it is also twinned with an equally beautiful part of the Bruce Trail in Ontario, Canada as a mark of friendship and cooperation between our two trails.

- Distance: 6 miles. Duration: 2 ½ -3 ½ hours. Difficulty: Moderate – some stiles and moderate slopes'.
- You can download the map from www.nationaltrail.co.uk

You might also like to know that the National Trust has mapped a walk to the south and south west of Haresfield Beacon making it possible to have a figure of eight starting/finishing at Shortwood car park. Known as the 'Haresfield Beacon Walk', it's about 4.8 miles (7.7 km) in length and described as 'challenging'.

- You can download the map from www.nationaltrust.org.uk

Car Parking
- For the start at Cam Peak, see the end point on the previous stage.
- At Haresfield, there's a small National Trust pay and display car park shown on the OS Map (SO 832 086); there is additional space in a smaller car park further along the lane.

Chapter 8
The 'Queen' and two beacons beckon
Haresfield to Coopers Hill

Apart from a few gaps here and there, around three quarters of this stage's route is in woodland. You'll not want for other interests, however. Because, in the gaps, you'll find yourself on top of two Cotswold hills with their famous beacons and associated hill forts. You can have lunch in the town known as the 'Queen of the Cotswolds' with its conservation area and literally hundreds of listed buildings. You can also visit its famous churchyard where you'll feel obliged to try to count the yew trees. Also on route, you pass some Rococo gardens and an abbey that isn't the ruin that others on the trail are. Journey's end brings you to yet another famous and, perhaps, the steepest of the Cotswold Hills, renowned for an annual cheese rolling event of all things. You might also like to know that you are roughly half way along the Cotswold Way on this stage.

Haresfield Beacon - more than just views

Assuming you're starting at the National Trust's Shortwood car park, go up to the Topograph to remind yourself of what you saw at the end of the previous stage: stunning views towards the Severn estuary, Forest of Dean and the Brecon Beacons. Then it's down to the left and up to Haresfield Beacon with yet more gorgeous views.

As in so many other cases, it's not just the views that matter. Haresfield Beacon and Broadbarrow Green are sites of ancient British and Roman encampments. Indeed, these encampments were a part of a chain of fortresses explicitly mentioned by Tacitus, the Roman historian, as having been raised by Ostorius Scapula between the Severn and Avon Rivers: old British works adapted by the Romans to their own requirements. It is also thought the name of the village Harescombe is derived from a combination of the Celtic term 'cwm' (valley) and the Saxon term 'here' (army), thus the full meaning of 'Harescombe' would be 'the Army's Valley". In the words Historic England:

> *This monument, which falls into two separate areas of protection, includes a slight univallate hillfort, Romano-British settlement, cross dyke, bowl barrow and beacon all situated on the prominent summits of the Ring and Haresfield Hills which together form the watershed to a large number of tributaries to Daniel's Brook and the River Frome.*

> *Originally viewed as a single large hillfort bisected by a road, subsequent survey work in 1995 and re-evaluation now means a slightly different interpretation has been reached. On the western Ring Hill section is a slight univallate hillfort defined by a single rampart bank measuring up to 9.1m wide and 1.2m high with no clearly discernible outer ditch but evidence of artificially enhanced*

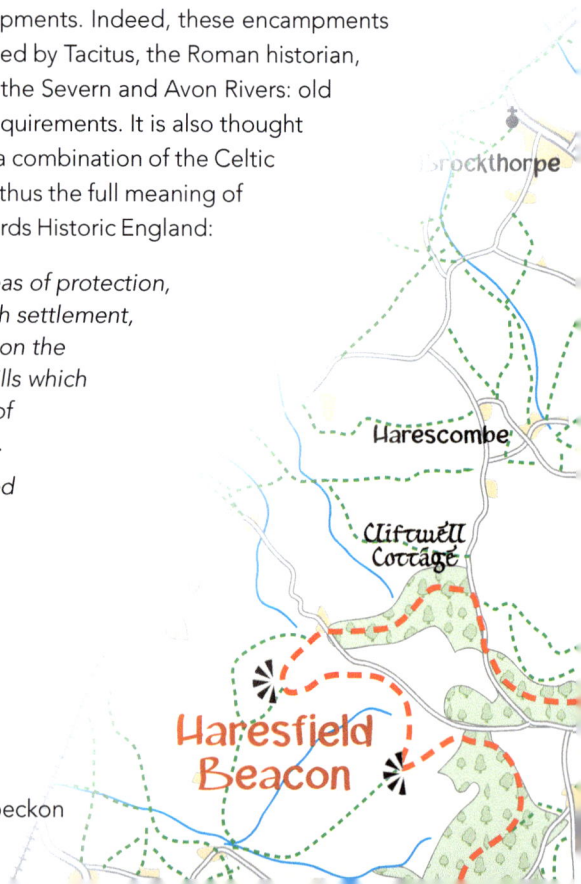

Brockworth

Gloucester

Cooper's
Hill

Upton
St Leonards

Great
Witcombe

Roman
Villa

Prinknash
Abbey

Buckholt Wood

Cranham

Painswick
Beacon

Sheepscombe

Edge

Painswick

Pitchcombe

natural scarps. Within this enclosed area chance finds of Roman remains were made in 1837 and included a rotary quern, pottery and animal bones, whilst a possible building was identified. The more recent survey confirmed occupation of this date which suggested an Iron Age hillfort had been re-used as a settlement in the Romano-British period.

Also in the centre of the enclosed area are two circular mounds of similar size being 18m in diameter and up to 2m high. One has a buried quarry ditch and is a bowl barrow and the other which supports a concrete triangulation pillar is actually 'Haresfield Beacon' and has commanding views over the surrounding countryside.

To the east the outer limits of the area are defined by 'The Bulwarks' originally seen as the outer defences of a much larger hillfort but now thought to represent a cross dyke. These earthworks survive as a single bank of up to 13.7m wide and 2.1m high with a ditch of up to 12m wide and 2.1m deep. The upper area of the hill tops has also been subject to periodic quarrying.

As for the 'beacon' in Haresfield Beacon, Historic England explains:

Beacons were fires deliberately lit to give a warning, by means of smoke by day and flame by night, of the approach of hostile forces. They were always sited in prominent positions, usually as part of a group, chain or line which together made up a comprehensive early warning system covering most of the country. Beacons were extensively used during the medieval period. Their use was formalised by 1325 and although some were used later, for example at the time of Monmouth's Rebellion in 1685 or during the Napoleonic wars, the system was in decay by the mid-17th century. Beacons were initially bonfires of wood or furze, but later barrels of pitch or iron fire baskets mounted on poles were used. The poles were occasionally set on earthen mounds. Access to the fire basket was by way of rungs set in the pole, or by a stone ladder set against the beacon.

Remember your latin - the inscription at Cliftwell Cottage

Cromwell's Stone and the entry into Painswick

After the beacon, you go round Haresfield Hill into woods. Not long after starting, you will be able to admire examples of the Cotswold Wardens' work to make the path at this point safer using riveting and handrails. Further on, going through Cliff Wood, you'll come across Cliffwell cottage (named after the well beside which it is set). Try to read the inscription on the well-head. It says: 'Whoer the Bucketful upwindeth, let him bless God, who water finest. Yet water here but small availeth. Go seek that well which never failest'.

Slightly further on near the entrance to Trump's Farm, you'll come face to face with 'Cromwell's Stone' - an asymmetrical arrangement of three large stones. Supposedly, it commemorates the lifting of the 'Siege of Gloucester' by Royalist forces on 5th September 1643 during the first English Civil War of 1643-1645. One problem is the date. The original inscription has worn away, but records show 'Siege of Gloucester, raised 5th September 1645' - i.e. two years later. Like passers-by have done for years, you may also wonder why, on this quiet path in the middle of nowhere and miles from Gloucester, there is such a stone and why it should bear Cromwell's name! Most likely the queries are down to the Niblett family who purchased the Haresfield Estate at the beginning of the 19th century and who are thought to have erected the monument. Perhaps, it's been suggested, the name 'Cromwell' is just being used as an all-embracing term for the Parliamentarian cause generally.

Hallidays Wood and Mailand's Wood are up next, with their disused quarries, followed by Rudge Hill Nature Reserve. Edge Common is a good place to restawile and again admire the views - in summer it's also an excellent place to see many species of butterflies, along with several varieties of orchid and herbs.

From the common, cross the A4173 to the Edgemoor Inn, which overlooks Painswick, and continue down. Not long after you'll come across the 'Halfway Stone' in one of the fields. You have, in other words, reached the halfway point on the Cotswold Way. Proceeding across more fields, you'll pass Washbrook Farm and Painswick's rugby pitches. As you come into Painswick on Edge Road, look out for the refurbished metal sign commemorating Toby Drake who helped to establish the Cotswold Way.

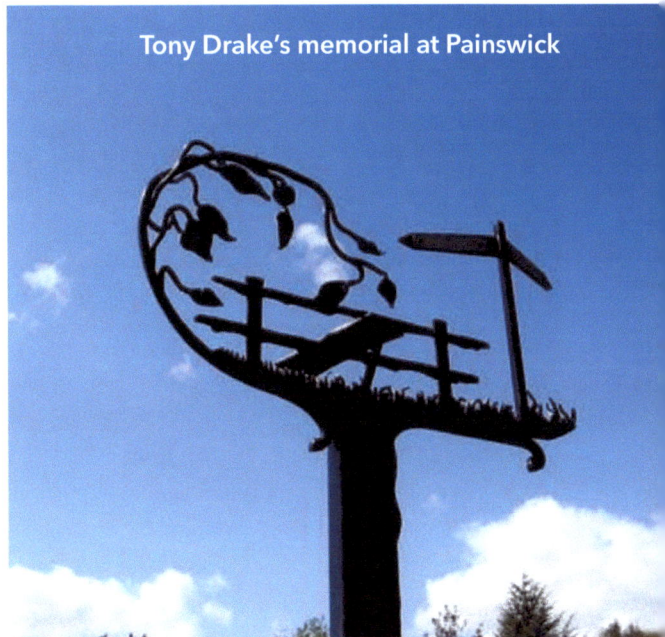

Tony Drake's memorial at Painswick

Painswick Post Office

Painswick - the Queen of the Cotswolds

Its Wikipedia entry tells us that Painswick initially developed during Anglo-Saxon times at the junction of two roads - an old road coming from what is now the Stroud area up past Wick Street and down Stepping Stone Lane (or thereabouts) into Painswick, and another old road that came from Bisley across the valley, along what is now Bisley Street and thence on to Gloucester. Painswick first appears in historical records in the Domesday Book of 1086, as 'Wiche' or 'dairy-farm'. It continues to appear by this name into the 13th century. The form 'Painswik' first appears in 1237 and, most likely, originates in the name of an earlier lord of the manor, Pain Fitzjohn, who died in 1137. At the time of Pain Fitzjohn, the manor house is thought to have been located on the site currently occupied by Court House and Castle Hale. It was described as a 'castellum' - a fortified mansion.

Painswick is often called The 'Queen of the Cotswolds'. It's not without good reason. Picture-perfect, it has the largest number of listed buildings of any of the towns on the Cotswold Way - at the last count, it was reckoned that there were nearly 400! Just opposite as you come in on Edge Road is the Lych Gate. Turn left onto New Street and there's the Falcon Hotel, which boasts the oldest bowling green in the country - these greens were once a common feature of inns and pubs. A few doors along is the Post Office, which is housed in the only exposed half-timbered building in the town. This is reputedly the oldest building in England to hold a post office. New Street itself was built in 1428.

Painswork, as the Painswick Local History Society emphasises, is a 'wool town'. Unlike Wotton and Campden, however, it was not so much the sale of wool that was to the fore, though a charter for a weekly market was granted in 1253. Rather it was cloth making that made the difference. The origins of the industry in Painswick are uncertain. Initially, though, the industry would have been small-scale cottage based. Later, waterpower from the relatively fast flowing Painswick Stream and its tributaries helped to revolutionise production. Some nineteen mills have been identified along these streams, though not all were continuously involved in cloth manufacture, with nearly 30 cloth mills in Painswick Parish overall.

The industry's heyday was from about the middle of the 15th century to the early 19th century. The several processes involved left an indelible imprint on the town, which the Society's website enables us to see photographs of in the eBook edition.

Thus, there were barns to store the wool and round towers for the wool to hang to dry after being washed. The room at the rear of Byfield House in Bisley Street was a wool barn in the 17th and 18th centuries. The 3-storey tower in Kemps Lane, now used as a workshop, was built in the 18th century.

On Bisley Street, you'll also find houses from the 14th century such as The Chur and Byfield House, that still show two so-called 'donkey doors'. These doors may seem extraordinarily wide by today's standards, but there is a reason for this width: they were built to allow a donkey laden with panniers of wool to pass through.

Cottages for mill workers were sometimes built beside the mill, as at Damsells Mill, which dates from 1674. A cloth mill until the 1820s, it then became a flour mill and is now a private house, with the water wheel still standing inside the building. Many of the once-mill workers' cottages, however, are to be found close to the market in Vicarage Street. Once regarded as the slum of Painswick, the cottages have been renovated in recent years.

As for the mills where the finishing processes produced the smooth broadcloth, there's the 17th century King's Mill, built on the site of a 15th century mill; this was a cloth mill until the middle of the 19th century and then a pin mill, its 30-foot long weaver's window being one of the longest in Gloucestershire. Savory's Pin Mill remained a working mill until closing in 1982.

There are also the fine houses that the prosperity of the clothiers in the 17th and 18th centuries made possible, several of which are still private residences. One example is Painswick Mill House by Painswick Stream, which dates from 1634. The mill made cloth until the 19th century, when it became a silk mill and then a pin mill. The sluice gates are still used to control the flow of the stream. Upstream from Painswick Mill is Cap Mill, which specialised in making the caps worn by workers in the cloth industry to denote their occupation. The mill house has a weaver's mark above the porch with the date 1678 and the initials of the clothier. Washbrook Mill was a corn mill then a cloth mill. A tablet in the wall of the house is dated 1691.

Several clothiers built their houses in the centre of Painswick and not next to their mills. Court House was built about 1604 for Thomas Gardner. The house stands on what is thought to have been the site of a former Manor House where the Manor Courts were held. Thomas Gardner sold the house to Dr John Searman, the Diocesan Chancellor who added the south-west wing. The north wing was built in the 1930s. Inside the house, there is 17th century paneling; the carved stone urn surmounts a gatepost in the grounds of Dover House which was probably built for a member of the Loveday family of clothiers. The house dates from about 1720 and is considered to be a perfect example of a small early Georgian variety.

Several old properties were restored or enlarged during the 17th century. Sheephouse, the property once occupied by the Sheep Bailiff was rebuilt and the dovecote added. The south wing was built in the early 18th century. Holcombe House was rebuilt for a clothier in the late 17th century; it was restored and enlarged in the 1920s. One of the 'new' buildings of the 17th century was Wick Street House which stands at the old main road between Painswick and Stroud. It was built for Giles Fletcher,

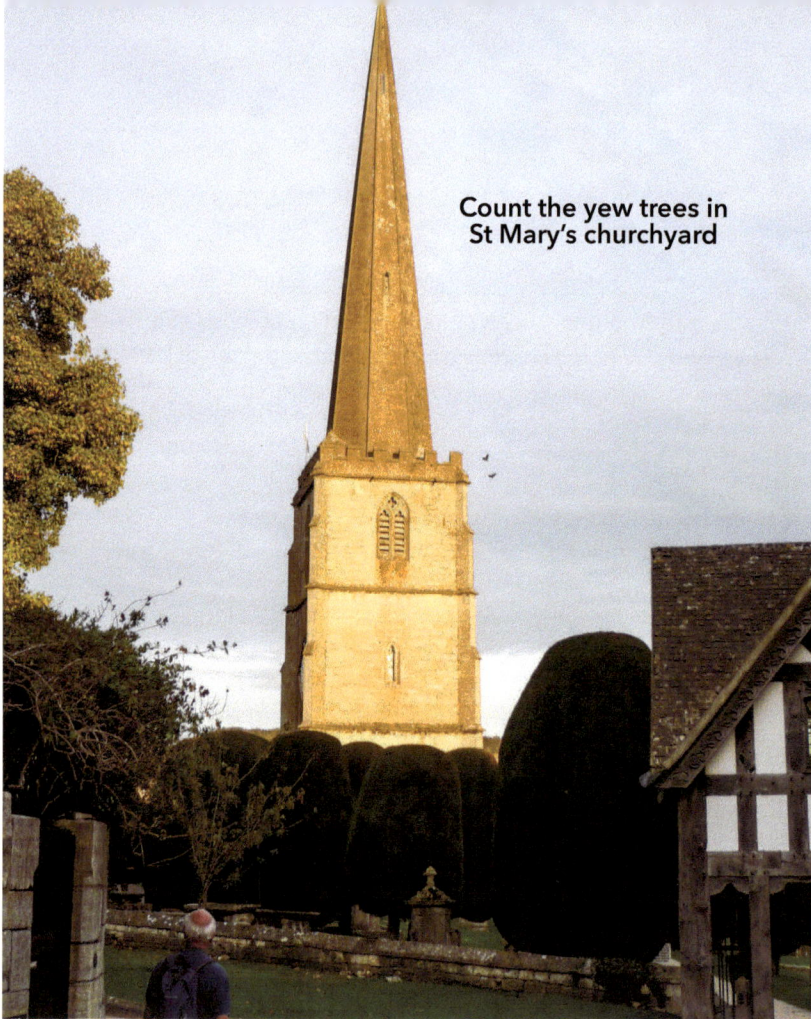

Count the yew trees in St Mary's churchyard

a clothier and Constable of the Manor; his initials and the date (1633) are carved beside the weaver's mark above the front door.

As well as enabling us to experience Painswick online, the Painswick Local History Society has very helpfully installed a set of six history information boards around the town, each of them introducing different aspects of Painswick's history. You'll find them in the following locations:

- Stamages Lane Car Park
- Victoria Square
- The Stocks
- Friday Street
- Bisley Street
- New Street.

You can also read them here on the eBook edition.

As in the case of Wotton-under-Edge, cloth making in Painswick declined with the coming of steam power and the growing importance of transport links such as the Stroudwater canal several miles further south. Some of the mills moved to other products that could be made with the help of water power. Fortunately, as in the case of Wotton-under-Edge and Chipping Campden, the die had been cast. The town had been made what it is.

St Mary's and its church yard - why it attracts so many visitors

Undeniably attractive though many of the buildings are, one of the most visited is the parish church of Painswick, St Mary's. It's not so much its architectural features that stand out, however. It also isn't normally listed in the wool churches like St James in Chipping Campden. The earliest parts, St Peter's Chapel, the north aisle and inner chancel, are thought to have been built between 1377 and 1401, possibly adjoining or replacing a Saxon or Norman church. The present nave and tower were started in 1480 or thereabouts, the spire added in about 1632, with the south aisle following in 1741.

Look closely at the tower and you'll see the scars of cannonballs left by a bombardment in 1643 during the first English Civil War. At the time, Parliamentary troops took refuge in the church, but were forced out by a combination of cannon fire and burning brands wielded by Royalist soldiers. These soldiers were said to have gathered at the shop across from St. Mary's, where they lit their torches before storming the church. That shop is, appropriately, called, 'The Fiery Beacon Gallery'.

A second feature is the churchyard. It's criss-crossed with paths and graced with fine elegant tombstones, most of which date from before 1860, when the churchyard was closed for burials. The tombstones come in many shapes and sizes including 'pedestal tombs' and the well preserved 'Table Top Tombs', which local stonemasons elaborately decorated, though some of the detail has been lost with the passage of time on the soft limestone. You can check each tomb yourself, but Tim Copeland gives us an overview in his archaeological guide:

> A wide variety of designs, progressing from the upright headstones to the massive horizontal ledger, the chest, the pedestal and the 'tea caddy', are to be found in the churchyard. The inscribed names reflect the social history of Painswick, and the vigorous commercial life of the town is represented by mill owners, salters, a timber merchant, an army captain, a druggist, an apothecary, a nurseryman, bakers, tallow chandlers, farmers, butchers, cordwainers, and maltsters, though only one servant is represented.

There is also the abundance of yew trees that draw the most attention. These probably go back to the late 1700s. The exact number, at the risk of making an awful pun, is for you to count. Why bother? Legend has it that the churchyard will never have more than 99 yew trees and that, should a 100th grow, the Devil would pull it out. Trouble with that is the plan of the churchyard included in the church's own public leaflet shows 100. Also, according to the Victoria and Albert Museum, a count of the trees showed there to be 103. Another legend says that the trees are uncountable, the other, that there are 99 trees, and if a hundredth was to be planted, the devil would shrivel it. So take your pick!

St. Mary's is also well known for its annual 'Clypping ceremony'. On the first Sunday after 19 September, there is an annual festival called 'Feast Sunday'. Three customs were historically followed: feasting, drinking and disorderly conduct; clipping the church; and eating 'dog pie'. The ceremony known as 'clipping the church' involves mostly children, but also adults, who join hands, dance around and 'embrace'. Clipping the church and eating dog pie are customs that have been revived and continue to be practised. The 'dog pie' is not made of dog meat, but the custom is based upon plum pie baked with a porcelain china dog. You might justifiably surmise that this September ceremony had to do with trimming the yew trees, but you'd be wrong. The ceremony involves the children of the parish embracing the church, singing hymns, and carrying nosegays of flowers.

On to Painswick Beacon

About half a mile north of the village as you leave Painswick behind, you pass Painswick House on your left with its six acres of formal and informal gardens known as Painswick Rococo Garden. The garden, which may more properly be called a 'pleasure ground', is a rare survivor of the very brief rococo period in English garden design. The house was built in 1735 by Charles Hyett and originally called 'Buenos Aires' because of the fine air in Painswick. The Rococo Garden was constructed about ten years later and captured in a painting by Thomas Robbins. The original fell into disuse, but the painting enabled their accurate reconstruction from the late 1980s.

As you go along the edge of the golf course, you may notice on the map that the area across to the right of the A46 is called 'Paradise'. Tradition has it that, while the Royalists were encamped in Painswick, King Charles I went up to the Painswick Beacon and, seeing the beautiful valley to his east, said 'This must be Paradise'.

After emerging from the wood, the trail takes you up to reach Painswick Beacon just beyond Catbrain Quarry. Here you'll find some 250 acres of common land offering excellent views towards the winding river Severn, Malvern Hills, Severn Crossing Bridges and the Welsh Mountains. The Beacon's Topograph at the peak, incidentally, was donated by the Cotswold Voluntary Wardens in 2008 to celebrate their 40th anniversary.

Also to be found are the ramparts of an Iron Age hill fort. Here's Historic England's description:

> The monument includes a large multivallate hillfort situated on the summit of a prominent hill which forms the watershed between the valleys of the River Twyer, Painswick Stream and Wash Brook. The hillfort survives as a roughly triangular enclosed area defined on the west and south sides by three rampart banks with two medial ditches and to the north by a natural scarp augmented by a single rampart bank. There is an inturned entrance to the south east and a simple entrance to the north west with an old trackway. In total the hillfort covers an area of approximately 8.8ha.

> The subject of recent extensive earthwork repairs and restoration, the interior, despite extensive past quarrying, has produced chance finds of Iron Age and Romano-British date, including pottery.

Historic England goes on to tell us that the hillfort is known locally by a number of different names: 'Painswick Beacon', 'Painswick Hill Camp', 'Kimsbury Hillfort' and 'Castle Godwyn'. It's also believed to have been occupied in 1643 as an outpost by the army of King Charles I during the siege of Gloucester.

Prinknash - the Abbey that survived dissolution

After the Beacon, the trail takes you through three woods in the direction of Cooper's Hill and the end point of the stage: Popes Wood, Upton Wood, and Brockworth Rough Park. En route, you'll see the signs for Prinknash Abbey on your left. Prinknash Abbey is a Roman Catholic monastic community of men. As its Wikipedia entry explains, the land known as Prinknash (locally pronounced 'Prinich' or 'Prinish') has been associated with the Benedictines for nearly 900 years. In 1096 the Giffard family, who had come to England with William the Conqueror, made a gift of the land to the Abbot of Saint Peter's in Gloucester. In 1339, the Prinknash Abbey website tells us, the Bishop of Worcester granted

Prinknash Abbey

a licence to the Abbot and his 'manor of Princkenasch', making it clear that Prinknash was an abbatial manor and had a chapel where Mass was said.

On dissolution, the abbey 1539 was rented from the Crown by Sir Anthony Kingston, who was to provide 40 deer annually to King Henry VIII, who used the house as a hunting lodge. Having passed through the hands of several local dignitaries over the next few centuries, Prinknash Park eventually came into possession of the Dyer-Edwardes family.

In 1924, Thomas Dyer-Edwardes, the then head of the family, became a Catholic and invited the Benedictines of Caldey to make a foundation at Prinknash Park. The gift of Prinknash seemed providential and so they accepted, eventually selling their island of Caldey to the Cistercians.

There was, however, a twist to the story. Mr. Dyer-Edwardes died in Naples in February 1926 making the Deed of Gift legally inoperative. His grandson who inherited, the Benedictines of Prinknash explain, could have excused himself from the undertaking, but 'with a generosity and disinterestedness, which the community will ever gratefully remember, he did in fact honour his grandfather's wishes in this matter'. A new Deed of Conveyance was made out in August 1928 and signed by him, in which the Grantor conveys to the Trustees 'all that messuage or tenement known as Prinknash Park, with the stabling, electric light house, and the chapel, pleasure grounds and lands, containing in all 27 acres, 1 rood, and 21 perches'. Sadly, the death duties were such that the donor was forced to sell all the valuables in the house before handing it over.

Entrance to the Prinknash estate, says the Prinknash Abbey website, is free and members of the public are invited to enjoy 'the peaceful atmosphere of the Prinknash Monastery Shop and Cafe and sample the local homemade cakes and refreshments'. Also men can stay at the monastery - Benedictine monasteries have been welcoming guests for hundreds of years and Prinknash says it's pleased to continue that tradition. Indeed, it is integral to their way of life. If you would like to stay or share in a time of prayer and quiet reflection then you simply have to contact the Guest Master who will be happy to provide further details.

Cooper's Hill - it really is that steep!

Coopers Hill - anyone for cheese rolling?

Our destination on this stage is the small car park at the foot of Cooper's Hill. At the risk of stating the obvious, the slope of this 200-yard/183 metres-long hill is extremely steep - the idea of running down it in pursuit of a bouncing cheese is just mind boggling! But that's what's been happening for many years.

To paraphrase the Wikipedia entry, the Cooper's Hill Cheese-Rolling and Wake is an annual event held on the Spring Bank Holiday. Participants race down the hill after a round of Double Gloucester cheese is sent rolling down it. The first person over the finish line at the bottom of the hill wins the cheese. The competitors are aiming to catch the cheese; however, it has around a one-second head start and can reach speeds up to 70 miles or 110 kms per hour, enough to knock over and injure a spectator. In the 2013 competition, therefore, a foam replica replaced the cheese for reasons of safety, with the winner given the prize of an actual cheese after the competition.

The event was traditionally held by and for the people who live in the local village of Brockworth, but now people from all over the world take part. *The Guardian* called it a 'world-famous event', with winners coming from Canada, Australia, New Zealand, and Nepal.

Two possible origins have been suggested for this strange event. The first is that it evolved from a requirement for maintaining grazing rights on the common. The second, and more pagan, is that bundles of burning brushwood were rolled down the hill to represent the birth of the New Year. Anyway, although reckoned to be an old tradition, the first written evidence of cheese rolling is found in a message written to the Gloucester town crier in 1826.

Cotswold Way Circular Walk

This stage gives us another of the twelve Cotswold Way Circular Walks. It's No 7 and called 'Cranham, Cooper's and the Beechwoods'. In the words of the National Trails website:

'This beautiful little walk shows you around one of England's most treasured habitats, beech woodlands, and leads you to the site of perhaps the Cotswolds' most iconic and intriguing tradition, cheese-rolling. Follow these four short miles and discover the cathedral-like calm of Buckholt Wood, richly carpeted by bluebells in May, and wonder at the dizzy heights of Cooper's hill where for hundreds of years the foolhardy have risked their necks for cheese and glory…

- *Distance: 4 miles. Duration: 2 – 3 hours. Difficulty: Easy. No stiles, but some moderately steep sections'.*
- You can download the map from www.nationaltrail.co.uk

Car Parking
- For the start at Haresfield, see the end point on the previous stage.
- At Cooper's Hill, there's a small car park at its base (SP 8928 1480) just off the A46, with a couple of lay-bys on the A46 close by shown on the Harvey National Trail Cotswold Way map.

Chapter 9
Not just views from on high
Coopers Hill to Seven Springs

You have a great mix of walking and sites to see on this stage. You'll be spending several miles in or by the side of woods, much of which is in shady sunken hollows. You will pass the remains of several Neolithic sites, along with an outstanding Roman villa. A country park awaits you for lunch with gorgeous views in every direction, followed by a famous hill with its Victorian quarries that were so influential in the building of Cheltenham that lies below. You will also be able to find out about a Celtic mirror, a pioneering air balloon site and a 'devil's chimney'. You may even be able to make a contribution to finding the 'missing link' in a controversial major road rerouting.

A hidden gem - Great Witcombe Roman villa

As with the previous stage, you have long stretches of walking through or beside woodland on this stretch of the trail. To begin with, there is Cooper's Wood that is a remnant of ancient beech woodland with a good flora, particularly bluebells and several orchid species. It sits at the foot of the hill of the same name from where you can get good views of Brockworth to your north. Brockworth is where they built Hawker Hurricanes in World War II - in the first 12 months they delivered 1,000 and in the next two years another couple of thousand. Production was then switched to building Hawker Typhoons. On 8 April 1941 the first test flight of Sir Frank Whittle's Gloster E28/39 with a single turbo-jet engine took off from the Brockworth airfield to be followed later by the twin-engined Gloster Meteor. The speed of the Meteor, they say, enabled it to fly alongside V1 flying bombs and tip them off course to crash before they could bomb London. In 1945 the Meteor gained a world speed record of 606 mph (975 km/h) and it was eventually put into service by 12 nations.

After Cooper's Wood, there are several miles to go through Witcombe Wood. Here the canopy is pretty dense being dominated by beech, along with ash, sycamore and oak. Occasionally there are small clearings from where you can look across to Witcombe Park, a large area of green set upon a rolling hillside, and to the Witcombe Reservoirs.

If you're looking for some relief from the woodland walking, a mile or so into this stage and you will find a hidden gem:

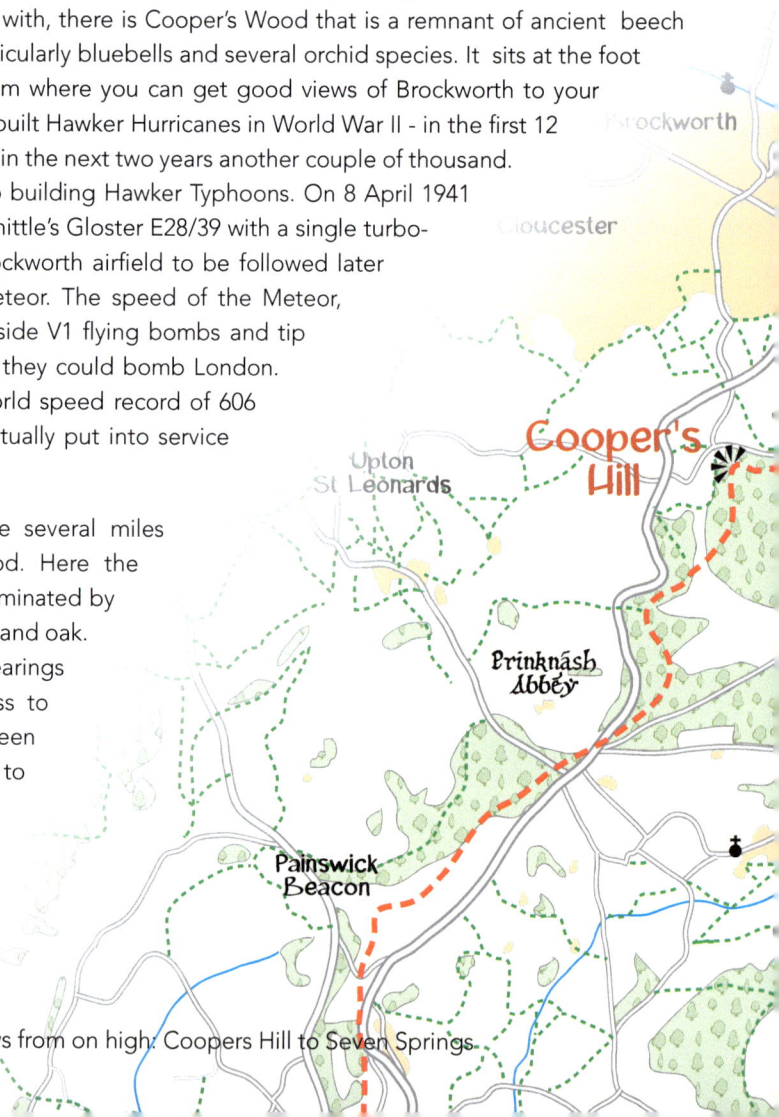

Cotswold Way ━ ━ ━
Public footpaths ┄┄┄┄┄
Viewpoint
For more detail see:
OS Explorer OL 179

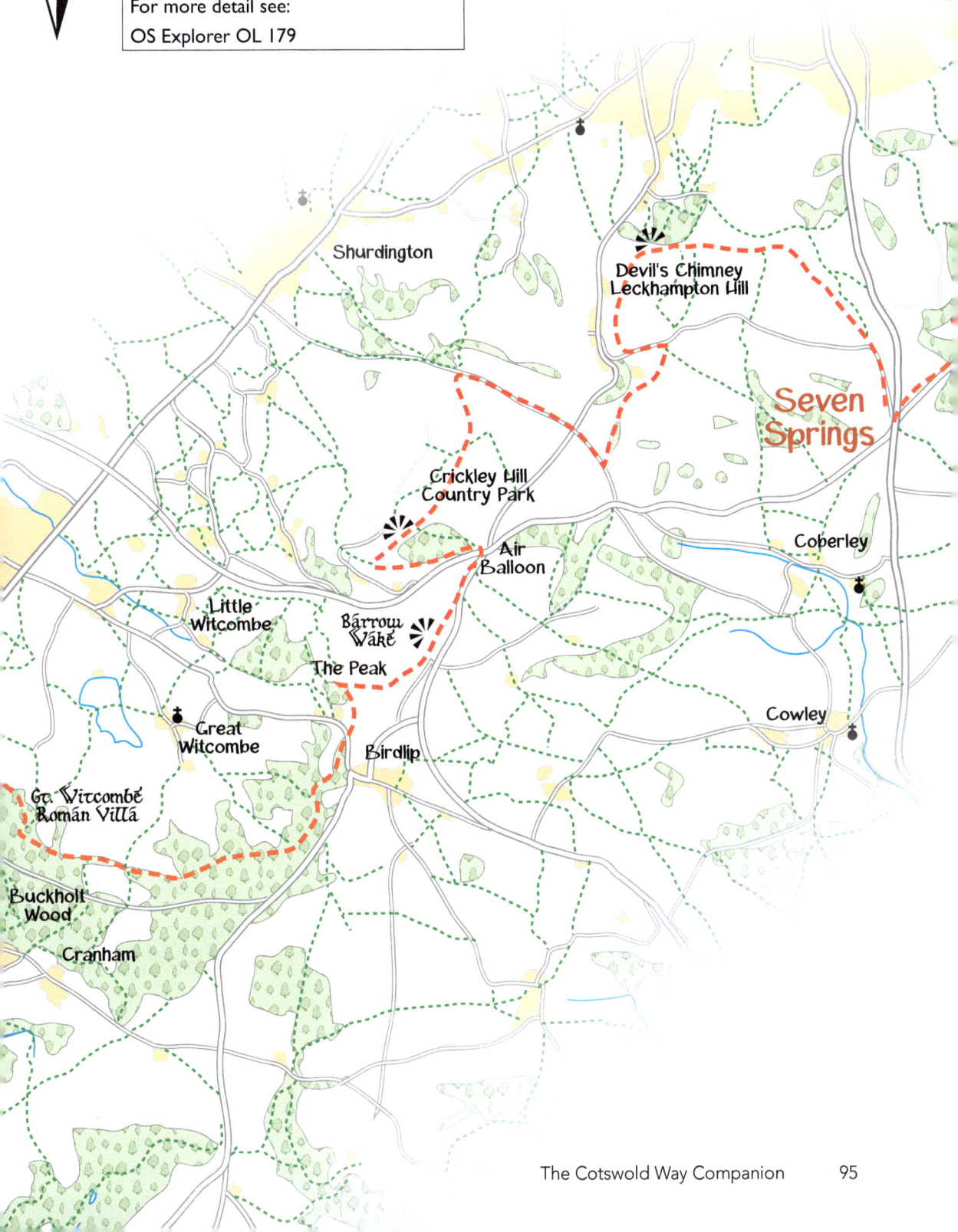

Shurdington

Devil's Chimney
Leckhampton Hill

Seven
Springs

Crickley Hill
Country Park

Coberley

Air
Balloon

Little
Witcombe

Barrow
Wake

The Peak

Cowley

Great
Witcombe

Birdlip

Gt. Witcombe
Roman Villa

Buckholt
Wood

Cranham

the one Roman 'villa' more or less on the Cotswold Way. As Chapter 2 has pointed out, the Cotswolds were home to many Villa Rustica. Introducing the monument at Great Witcombe, Historic England give us a good idea of what was entailed:

> Romano-British villas were extensive rural estates at the focus of which were groups of domestic, agricultural and occasionally industrial buildings. The term 'villa' is now commonly used to describe either the estate or the buildings themselves. The buildings usually include a well-appointed dwelling house, the design of which varies considerably according to the needs, taste and prosperity of the occupier. Most of the houses were partly or wholly stone-built, many with a timber-framed superstructure on masonry footings. Roofs were generally tiled and the house could feature tiled or mosaic floors, underfloor heating, wall plaster, glazed windows and cellars. Many had integral or separate suites of heated baths. The house was usually accompanied by a range of buildings providing accommodation for farm labourers, workshops and storage for agricultural produce. These were arranged around or alongside a courtyard and were surrounded by a complex of paddocks, pens, yards and features such as vegetable plots, granaries, threshing floors, wells and hearths, all approached by tracks leading from the surrounding fields. Villa buildings were constructed throughout the period of Roman occupation, from the first to the fourth centuries AD. They are usually complex structures occupied over several hundred years and continually remodelled to fit changing circumstances. They could serve a wide variety of uses alongside agricultural activities, including administrative, recreational and craft functions, and this is reflected in the considerable diversity in their plan.

> The least elaborate villas served as simple farmhouses whilst, for the most complex, the term 'palace' is not inappropriate. Villa owners tended to be drawn from a limited elite section of Romano-British society. Although some villas belonged to immigrant Roman officials or entrepreneurs, the majority seem to have been in the hands of wealthy natives with a more-or-less Romanised lifestyle, and some were built directly on the sites of Iron Age farmsteads.

According to English Heritage, which looks after the Great Witcombe site, the date ranges for the villa's building and occupation are largely based upon coins found during excavations of the site. It adds that the villa itself is sited in an unusual location – the unevenness of the terrain, which was riddled with small streams and natural springs, would seem to render it unsuitable for such a large dwelling. It is thought, however, that these springs would have been harnessed into water features in stylised gardens and that a cult of water nymphs may have been cultivated around this. This is supposition, though.

To cope with the difficult terrain, the building itself was constructed on four terraces, cut into the hillside and heavily buttressed, which are still evident on the gallery connecting the two main wings of the house. The architectural design of the villa differs greatly from similar dwellings from the same period, given that the main living quarters were in the large eastern wing, and a long gallery of little function connected this wing with the 'leisure wing' where the bath house and temple were located. This layout reflects the evolution of the house over time—the bath house wing was a later expansion—and a consideration of the spatial restrictions of the site.

The mosaics are the highlight and now housed inside modern buildings on site because they are so fragile. You can see photographs of them, though, if you go to the English Heritage website, together with some objects excavated at the villa. There were at least three mosaics at Great Witcombe. Two were relatively simple geometric designs of which only fragments survive. The most impressive mosaic, however, is the marine mosaic from the 'frigidarium' (cold room) of the baths. This mosaic depicts a greater variety of sea creatures than any other in Roman Britain. One is an electric ray, which is not seen on any other Roman Britain mosaic. Local stone and reused tiles were used for the mosaics, but the very small tesserae (tiles) indicate that the work was very expensive, as small tiles take longer to lay and allow for finer detailed work. A master mosaicist probably completed the figures, perhaps working in a workshop or on a trestle table on site. When the mosaicist was happy with the design of the figures, they would have been transferred to the floor. A less skilled worker, perhaps an apprentice, would then have filled in the blank areas of mosaic around each figure.

Birdlip, The Peak and Barrow Wake

As you come to the end of Whitcombe Wood, you'll have Birdlip on your right, which is reckoned to be the highest village in the Cotswolds. Birdlip itself isn't on the trail, but you can make an optional detour to enjoy its pub (The Royal George). You may be wondering about the name. Ancient place-names often referred to features in the landscape, so Birdlip may have originally got its name due to its position - in the sense of a steep place from which only a bird could safely 'leap'. In medieval times Birdlip was spelt 'Brydelep' which may have come from two Old English words - 'bridd' (a bird) and 'hlep' (a leap). Another suggestion is that the name came from 'bride's leap': there may have been a folk-tale involving a bride flinging herself down the cliff in a desperate bid to avoid marrying the man her father had selected!

Just before Birdlip, and one km south of Crickley Hill and it's welcoming country park, you'll come to the 'Peak'. As well as being a great view point, excavations in the early 1980s confirmed that, on this flat promontory of the Cotswold escarpment overlooking the Severn Valley, there was a Neolithic enclosure referred to as 'Peak Camp' or 'Birdlip Camp'. Here's the summary of the report of Tim Darvill and his colleagues that appeared in the *Proceedings of the Prehistoric Society*:

> *Although heavily eroded by quarrying the site can be reconstructed as having two concentric arcs of boundary earthworks forming an oval plan which was probably open to the north where a steep natural slope defined the edge of the site. A section through the outer boundary showed four main phases of ditch construction, at least one causewayed. An extensive series of radiocarbon dates shows construction began in the late 37th century BC and probably continued through successive remodellings into the 33rd century BC or beyond. An internal ditch or elongated pit situated in the area between the inner and outer boundary earthworks had a similar history. Where sampled, the ditch and internal feature were rich in material culture, including a substantial assemblage of plain bowl pottery; flint implements and working waste; animal remains dominated by cattle but including also the remains of a cat; human foot bones; slight traces of cereal production; a fragment of a Group VI axe; part of a sandstone disc; and a highly unusual shale arc pendant of continental type. It is suggested that the ditch fills represent selectively redeposited midden material from within the site that started to accumulate in the late 5th or early 4th millennium BC. The construction and use of Peak Camp is contemporary with activity on Crickley Hill, and the two sites probably formed components of a single complex. Its use was also contemporary with the deposition of burials at local long barrows in the 'Cotswold-Severn' tradition which are linked by common ceramic traditions and the selective deposition of human body parts.*

After the 'Peak' is another well known viewpoint enabling you to see the Malvern Hills, the Severn Vale, together with distant glimpses of Wales. Now known as 'Barrow Wake', the whole site is designated as a Site of Special Scientific Interest (SSSI) and is also registered common land. The unimproved limestone grasslands support more than 100 different species of wild flowers, including rare orchids. Twenty two species of butterfly are found on the site including national rarities like the Chalk Hill Blue and Duke of Burgundy.

Barrow Wake derives its name from the discovery in 1879, by workmen quarrying for stone of a late Iron Age burial (c. 50 AD). In the simple stone tomb they discovered three skeletons. Associated with the central figure, that of a woman aged about thirty years, was a rich array of grave goods including an ornamented bronze mirror that has become internationally famous - it's become known as the 'Birdlip Mirror'. Details about the discovery and other points of interest in the area are given at the viewpoint information panels which you will find beside the footpath near the car park. The finds themselves, which are said to represent some of the finest surviving examples of British Celtic metalwork, are displayed in Gloucester City Museum.

If you look carefully, on the flat part of the hill, you can see the remains of a defensive wall which is about 2500 years old. Originally it was over five metres high and may have had a walkway along the top. Archaeologists think it defended an early Iron Age settlement which was later destroyed and the wall burnt around 500 BCE.

The Air Balloon and the A417 'missing link' saga

It is difficult to tell you what to expect as you follow the trail from Barrow Wake to Crickley Park. It's here that the trail has to negotiate a roundabout junction where the A417, a major road between Swindon and Gloucester via Cirencester, meets the A436, the two roads together forming a de facto bypass of Cheltenham between Oxford and Gloucester. It's meant to be a high-quality route between the M4 and M5 motorways.

As Highways England explains, the problem is that, as well as being a difficult crossing for walkers, the junction is a notorious accident blackspot; from 1999 to 2014 there were an estimated 340 casualties. In March 2019 Highways England proposed improvements that would include demolition of the pub, ruling out a junction at it as the local geography and steep hills nearby would make it impossible to build a high-quality road meeting modern safety standards. The road couldn't be routed anywhere else as it would cut through Barrow Wake, which is a SSSI. Highways England stated that it would talk to landowners and assess the social impact of the pub's demolition in a further design stage.

If the Air Balloon is demolished, it will be a great pity - and not just because it won't be able to offer you a welcome break. The pub, which opened in 1784, is thought to have been known as the Balloon by 1796, being renamed the Air Balloon in 1802. This is believed to be in recognition of one of the first British balloon flights: the launching of a small hydrogen balloon by Edward Jenner on 2 September 1784, which flew from Berkeley Castle to Kingscote and then on to a field near Birdlip. Its significance is that it was only one year after the pioneering flights of the Montgolfier brothers' hot air balloon and Jacques Charles' hydrogen balloon in Paris. By 1856, the landlord was brewing beer on-site. The premises were part of the Cowley Manor Estate until some time early in the twentieth century. The pub was bought by Greene King in 2004.

Crickley Hill Country Park

Let's assume you've managed to navigate the A417 crossing safely. Next up is Crickley Hill Country

Park, which is jointly owned by the National Trust and the Gloucestershire Wildlife Trust: it sits on a prominent spur of the Cotswold escarpment and is a distinctive landmark that overlooks the Severn Vale. There are also magnificent views towards Robinswood Hill and May Hill, and the Brecon Beacons and Black Mountain beyond.

As the National Trust emphasises, Crickley Hill is 'more than just a view'. Most of the park is designated as a SSSI. It's rich in wildlife and boasts a wide variety of habitats and plants. The limestone grassland is extremely rich in plants, which in turn support a large variety of insects, especially butterflies. Crickley Hill is also an important area of geological interest due to the Jurassic limestone outcrops around its boundary. The entire area of this natural wonderland is open to the public and there are also car parks, a cafe and toilets.

Part of the site also has 'Scheduled Ancient Monument' status, the excavation of which from 1969 to 1993 was one of the largest and longest-running of its kind in the UK. As the Crickley Hill online archive managed by the Crickley Hill Archaeological Trust reports, intensive excavations over a period of 25 years have produced evidence of human activity on the hill going back to 4,000 BCE and carrying on until the fifth century AD. The archaeological remains also point to a long and violent history. The first structures on the hill date back to 3500-2500 BCE and included an enclosure with a causeway. It was rebuilt several times, but after being aggressively attacked it was finally abandoned in the Neolithic Period, the enclosure and causeway being replaced by an Iron Age hill fort. This would have been a triangular patch on top of the hill covering almost nine acres and home to about 100 people. A rubble-cored timber laced rampart surrounded the settlement and a rock-cut, flat-bottomed ditch paralleled the rampart. Despite their best efforts to protect the fort, in the sixth century BCE, it was burned and abandoned. Over 400 arrowheads were discovered at its entrance, evidence of the bloody battle that took place.

Kirsten Jarrett, who was one of the archaeologists involved, picks up the story on The *Crickley Hill blog spot*:

> *Crickley Hill is an Iron Age hillfort in Gloucestershire that, like many in the west, probably had some late pre-Roman Iron Age activity after a period of abandonment, with sporadic activity during the early Roman period. It was perhaps during this time that occasional buildings were built on the top of the silted-up rampart ditches, and near to the main rampart entrance, although these structures alternatively belong to the later Roman period. A prehistoric ritual monument on the site - the 'Long Mound' - received votive deposits during the Roman period. There was also a possible rectangular Roman masonry structure near the western end of the hill.*

> *During the later Roman period (or possibly during the early 5th century), the hill was once again occupied, perhaps initially within the entrance for industrial activity (although again, this may belong to the earlier Roman phase). A village was built behind the rampart, mainly consisting of 'scooped' buildings arranged in rows; there was also evidence for industrial activity in this area. Buildings were sub-rectangular and sub-circular (perhaps in some cases, polygonal), and would perhaps have been built of cob or turf, with low thatch or turf roofs, and were only single roomed, although perhaps had some form of partition in one case.*

> *On the western end of the hill, a second, probably contemporaneous, settlement was built. This settlement was enclosed by a palisade fence (which perhaps had a 'guard-house' at the entrance), and contained a granary (itself enclosed within a separate fence), suggesting its higher status. The buildings of this settlement were more substantial, and probably timber-*

framed (sitting directly on the ground-surface), or post-built, resting upon post-pads. They were mainly circular, although the central building was rectangular, and partitioned. This building had a substantial hearth, as well as a number of cooking pits nexts to the front walls …

Both settlements were burnt down, and re-built to similar plans to, and nearby, the earlier buildings. However, they were burnt down again, and the settlement abandoned.

On to Seven Springs via Leckhampton Hill

After Crickley, you pass Ullenwood Manor and Saltley Grange. Ullenwood Manor is the home of the National Star College, an independent further education college and special school for people aged 16 to 25 with learning difficulties and physical disabilities. The college grounds include a private 18-hole golf course used by Ullenwood Manor Golfing Society. Cotswold Hills Golf Club, founded in 1902, is also located at Ullenwood.

Close by, you will pass an old army camp used during the two World Wars as a U.S. military hospital. After WW2, it became home to a formerly secret civil defence bunker intended as a Regional Seat of Government in the event of nuclear war. For three decades at the end of the 20th century, Ullenwood Camp was used each summer as accommodation for archaeologists engaged in excavating the site at nearby Crickley Hill. The site is now used as a training area by the Fire & Rescue Service.

The slightly further on Salterley Grange was built as a private house built around 1860. In 1908 Birmingham Town Council purchased and converted it into a tuberculosis sanatorium. In the 1930 it had 68 beds. After the creation of the National Health Service in 1948, the institution passed to the Cheltenham Hospital Management Committee, which continued to run it until the late 1960s. It has since been converted into flats.

Heading north towards Leckhampton Hill, you have extensive views over Cheltenham as the ridge looks down on Charlton Kings Common. Beware, though, It's a steep drop!.

As well as the views from its top, Leckhampton Hill is notable for two things. The first, and perhaps the most famous, is the 'Devil's Chimney', which is a limestone rock formation that stands above a disused quarry - it's wonderfully illustrated in Mark Richards' pen and ink drawing below. The slopes of Leckhampton Hill were quarried extensively to produce the stone needed for building in Cheltenham. This is above all true of the early 1800's and the rapid growth of Cheltenham below.

Legend holds that the rock formation is the chimney of the Devil's dwelling deep beneath the ground. Supposedly the Devil, provoked by the many Christian churches of the area, would sit atop Leckhampton Hill and hurl stones at Sunday churchgoers. However, the stones were turned back on him, driving him beneath the ground and trapping him there so he could not further harass the villagers. Now he uses the mass of stones as his chimney to let free the smokes of hell. Once upon a time, visitors to the 'Devil's Chimney' would leave a coin on top of the rock as payment to the Devil in exchange for his staying in his underground home and not leaving to create mischief and spread evil in the local area.

So what's the truth of the matter? There are two main explanations. One, suggested by 19th-century geologists, is that the 'Devil's Chimney's' strange shape could be put down to differential erosion, involving the softer outer rock being worn away to leave only the inner harder rock remaining. The trouble with this explanation, it's said, is that it doesn't tell us why there was a column of harder rock there in the first place.

It's the second explanation, therefore, which is more likely. It is that the 'Devil's Chimney' is the work of the quarrymen who were so prevalent on the hill. It could be that it came about by chance when blasting left it behind and the quarrymen decided to make it a feature. Or it could be that they left it behind as a joke! Either way, please note that climbing is prohibited!

The other significant feature of the hill is an Iron Age hill fort known as 'Leckhampton Camp'. All that can be seen today is a grassy bank and the remains of the timber-laced stone walls which formed the rampart providing the main defences for the site. Apparently, the rampart enclosed an area of about six acres with an entrance protected by two semi-circular guard chambers. Historic England offers us this description:

The monument includes a slight univallate hillfort and a bowl barrow within a square enclosure situated on the summit of the limestone plateau of the Cotswold escarpment overlooking the valley and tributaries of the River Chelt. The hillfort survives as an irregular shaped enclosure defined to the west by artificially enhanced scarps and on the remaining sides by a single rampart and ditch. Excavations in 1925 and 1969-71 showed the bank was up to 6m wide and 1.8m high and the ditch was 4.2m wide and 2.7m deep. The entrance is a complex inturned feature with two guard chambers. Chance finds over the years have indicated multiple phases of occupancy including the Iron Age, Romano-British, Anglo-Saxon and medieval periods.

To the east of the hillfort is a bowl barrow which survives as a circular mound up to 10m in diameter and 0.6m high with a hollowed centre. It is surrounded by a square enclosure defined by a 0.6m high bank. Excavations produced two human skeletons of possible Iron Age date but no direct link could be found between the barrow and the enclosure.

Finally, if you're walking on the Cotswold Way on Leckhampton Hill, do look out for an excellent example of the improvement work the CWA is helping to bring about. Mentioned in Chapter 1, it's around about SO 9523 1850. As you'll see from the photographs below, it involves a gate that was barely passable by a disabled outdoor mobility scooter or pushchair. The result was that a flat area to the side of the path was being used to bypass the gate, damaging the SSSI in the process.

The project, which was completed in September 2021 with the generous support of the HF Holidays Pathways Fund, now allows ALL users to have access to the majority of the Leckhampton Hill escarpment. Practically, it involved re-ramping, smoothing and grading a 2-3 metre wide path on both sides of the gate. Logistically, it meant having to deliver to the site 150 tonnes of limestone dust and Cotswold stone!

Before and after on Leckhampton Hill ...

Cotswold Way Circular Walk

This stage gives us another of the twelve Cotswold Way Circular Walks. It's No 4 and called The Leckhampton Loop. In the words of the National Trails website:

'This walk guides you around one of the most beautiful and varied stretches of the Cotswold Way. From rich grassland to peaceful woodlands, from Iron-Age remains to Victorian quarries, this route offers up a taste of the entire Cotswold landscape in 4 ½ sheltered and windswept miles.

- *Distance: 4 ½ miles. Duration: 2½ – 3hrs. Degree of difficulty: Moderate, no stiles but some steep sections'.*
- You can download the map from www.nationaltrail.co.uk

Car Parking

- For the start at the foot of Cooper's Hill, see the end point on the previous stage.
- At Seven Springs, you can park in the lay-by opposite the Hungry Horse near the junction of the A436 and A435 (nearest post code is GL53 9NG). Alternatively, try Seven Springs village. There are also car parks on Leckhampton Hill, useful if you want to walk the 'Leckhampton Loop' or around Crickley Country Park.

Chapter 10
The very best of nature trails
Seven Springs to Cleeve Common

Many of this book's chapters deal with people and the places and landscapes they helped to make. This one is first and foremost about natural phenomena. As well as the source of perhaps the UK's most famous river, you pass by three major woods in the hands of the Woodland Trust, the Gloucestershire Wildlife Trust and the Environment Agency respectively, along with a reservoir supporting an abundance of wildlife. Towards the end the walk is a world renowned Common that is a nationally important Site of Special Scientific Interest (SSSI) notable for its geology, habitats and botany as well as its archaeology; depending how much time you spend exploring it will determine whether you walk 8.5 miles (13.7 kms) or much longer. In any event, you will find trees, grasses and wildflowers of every description. If you're lucky, you'll come across orchids and a range of wildlife in its natural habitats, including the edible Helix Pomatia introduced by the Romans - which may or may not whet your appetite.

Seven Springs - the source of the Thames?

Your starting point, Seven Springs, features in the long-running argument over the true source of the River Thames. Since medieval times, the prevailing wisdom is that the source is at Thames Head near Kemble not far from Cirencester. However, beside a handy layby on the A436, there's a plaque which reads 'Hic tuus o Tamesine Pater septemgeminus fons'. For those of you who've forgotten your Latin, this translates into 'Here, O Father Thames, is your sevenfold spring'. According to the Coberley Parish Council notice posted on the plaque, 'Seven Springs is certainly one of the sources of the River Thames and is held by many to be the ultimate source'. This is because the site is the source of the River Churn, which flows into the Thames at Cricklade. As its location is further from the mouth of the Thames, the Churn headwater of the Thames adds some 14 miles or 22.5 kms to the length of the river flow. Furthermore, the springs at the site flow throughout the year, whereas those at the official source of Thames Head are only seasonal. The Churn/ Thames may therefore be regarded as the longest natural river flow in the United Kingdom, beating its nearest rival, the River Severn by 9 miles (14.5 Kms) – if much saltwater which well may be more of the sea than river, as place names like Southend-on-Sea attest, is taken as being river. If this is deemed to be correct, it would also be longer than the River Shannon (224 miles/360.5 kms), making it the longest river in the British Isles.

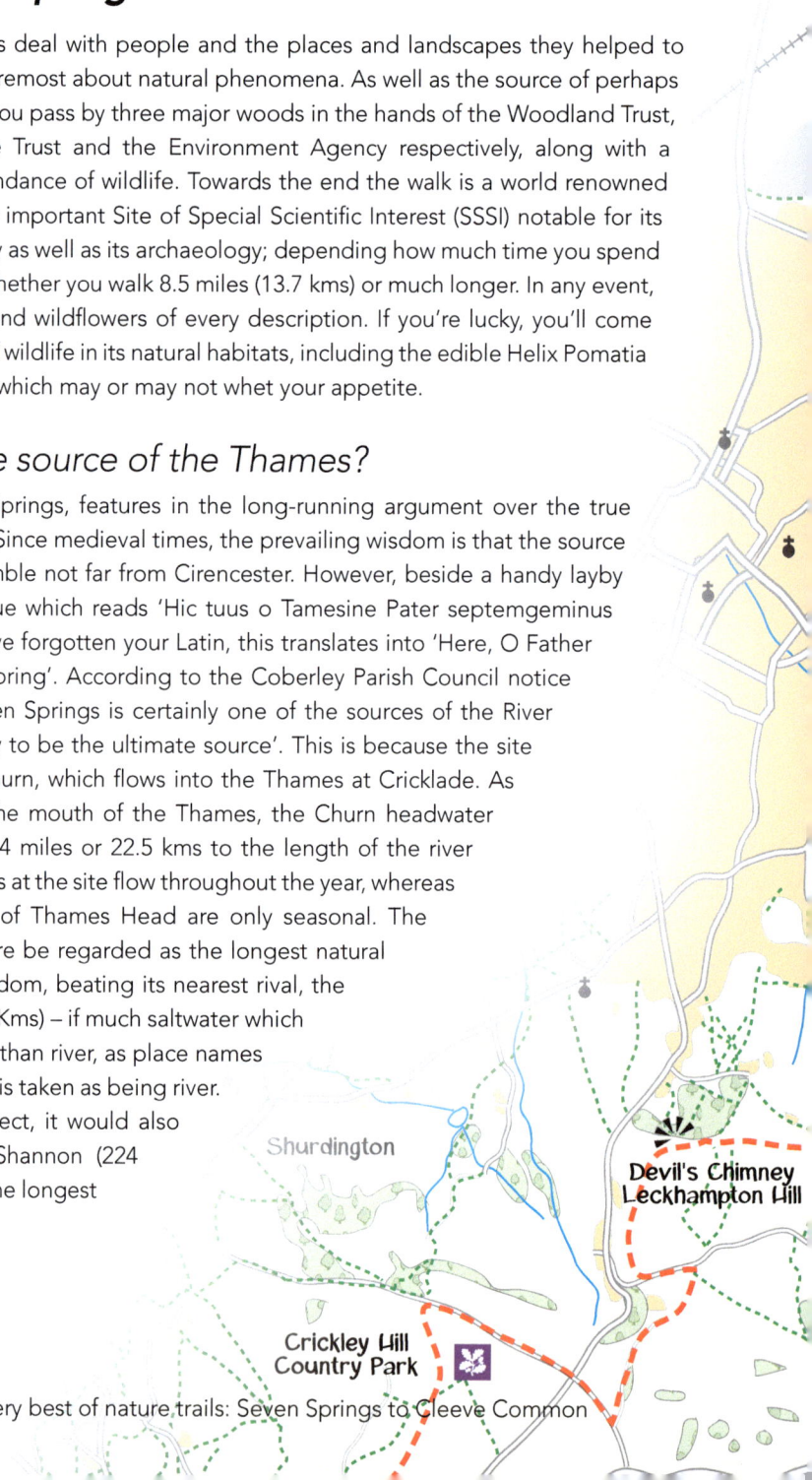

Shurdington

Devil's Chimney
Leckhampton Hill

Crickley Hill
Country Park

Postlip

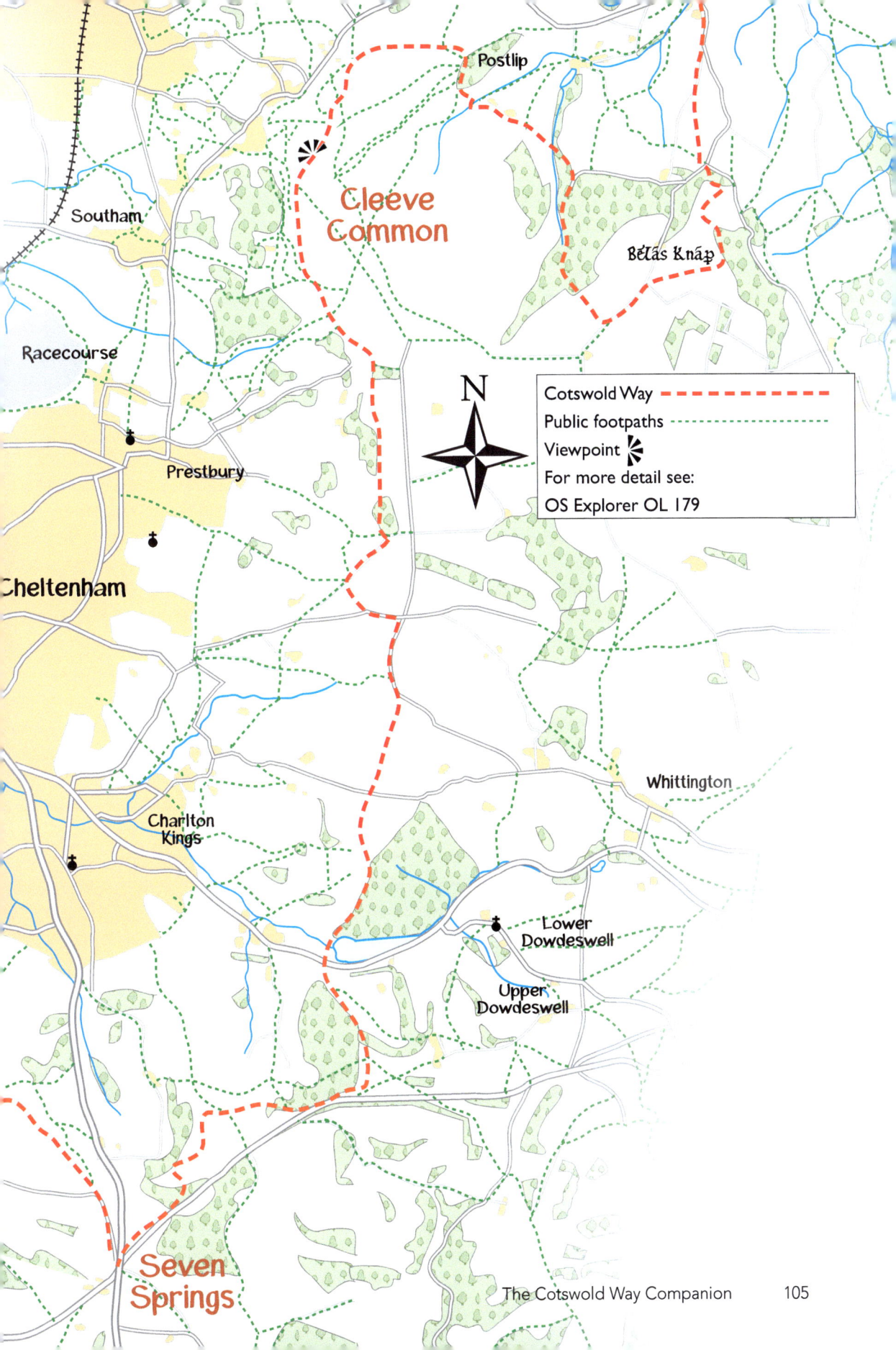

Cleeve
Common

Bélas Knáp

Southam

Racecourse

Prestbury

Cheltenham

Cotswold Way
Public footpaths
Viewpoint
For more detail see:
OS Explorer OL 179

Whittington

Charlton
Kings

Lower
Dowdeswell

Upper
Dowdeswell

Seven
Springs

Woods, hills and water

As you leave Seven Springs alongside the A436, you'll see Chatcombe Wood on the other side of the road. First mentioned in 1182, Chatcombe Wood was a major source of oak and ash trees for Gloucester Abbey for building repairs, 300 reported being reserved in 1524. Look out for kites and buzzards

Chatcombe Wood is followed by a couple of climbs in quick succession. The first is Wistley Hill and the second Ravensgate Hill. At the top, you're in for a treat: a magnificent view of Cleeve Hill to the North. You may also be able to see the Black Mountains, River Severn, Vale of Evesham and the Ski Slope at Gloucester. J.R. Tolkein is also reported to have taken inspiration from this view and used it for the structure of Middle Earth in his Lord of the Rings trilogy.

Thereafter things get a bit easier. Indeed, a couple of descents await you first east and then north through Lineover Wood to cross the A40 close to the Koloshi Restaurant/Pub opposite Dowdeswell Reservoir. Just before you reach the A40, you cross the line of the original Banbury to Cheltenham railway; this had a connection at Kingham (originally Norton Junction) to the Paddington-Worcester Line and, later, at Andoversford and Dowdeswell for the Midland and South Western junction railway, being heavily used during World War 2 to get military traffic to the South Coast. Local trains from Oxford to Cheltenham via Kingham, it seems, gave a later connection to Cheltenham from London than the direct route via Stroud - a feature appearing in detective novels with criminals being apprehended when it didn't seem to be possible.

Lineover Wood itself is a 20.3 hectare (50-acre) biological SSSI owned and managed by the Woodland Trust. It was first recorded around AD 800 as part of the Dowdeswell Estate, but it is likely to be much older. It therefore falls into the category of 'ancient' woodlands, i.e. areas of woodland that have persisted since 1600. Look out for the lime-coppice stool that has stood here for the best part of 1000 years; it's reached such an impressive age thanks to centuries of coppicing. On entering the wood there is a fairly steep descent (past an area of cleared woodland) with fine views to the East through the gaps in the trees. Towards the end of the climb there is a short path into an area where there is a collection of very large Beech trees (one of which reputedly has the largest girth in England).

Wildlife is plentiful in Lineover Wood. Look out for signs of the fallow, roe and muntjac deer which wander among the trees. You'll come across noisy flocks of long-tailed tits and may spot a woodcock or catch the mewing call of a buzzard as it circles high over the meadow. There is also a huge range of moths and butterflies to look out for, including the rare ghost moth.

Up next is Dowdeswell Reservoir, which together with two other adjacent areas (Residuum and Scobb's Grove), form a 23-acre nature reserve. The reservoir itself supports the native crayfish which is protected under the Wildlife & Countryside Act 1981 as well as being a major spawning ground for toads - warning signs are put up each year at migration time on the near-by A40. Apparently, there used to be a couple of toad tunnels from the south side of the A40 into the reservoir's grassland, but these have been removed. The main water also hosts many resident and wintering wildfowl such as Moorhen, Coot, Mallard and Little Grebe and Great Crested Grebes. Significant aquatic and grassland flora include Common Spotted Orchid, Pyramidal Orchid and Cowslip.

Keep an eye open, too, for the famous edible Helix Pomatia introduced by the Romans. The shell is creamy white to light brown with five to six whorls; the width of the shell is 30-50mm and 30-45mm in height. Also a protected species, the 'Roman snail' lifespan can be up to 35 years. Apparently, these large edible air-breathing 'gastropods' were highly prized and difficult to cultivate; before being cooked in butter and herbs, they were kept in jars and fed on milk until they could no longer fit in their own shell.

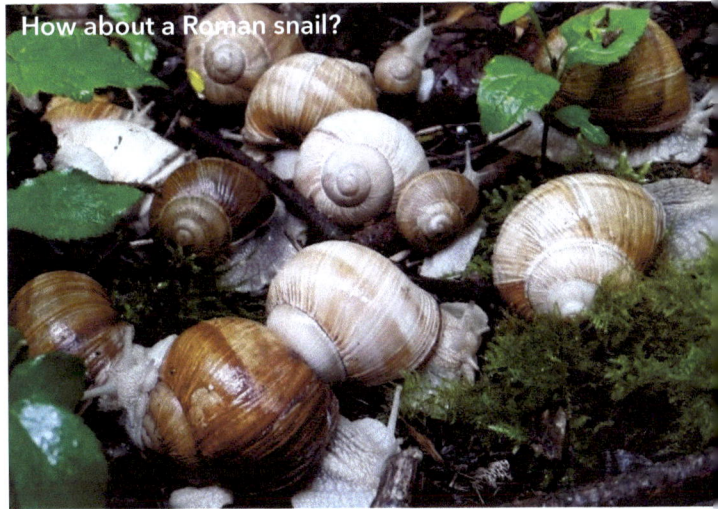
How about a Roman snail?

As for Dowdeswell Wood, its character was changed dramatically in the 1950s: many of the mature Oak, Ash, Beech, along with diseased Elms, being replaced with conifers. Replanting work has replaced conifers for broad-leaf. Extensive management work was carried out and a way-marked series of paths were created accessible from the Cotswold Way national trail. A good ground flora is present mostly in the broad-leaved areas. Bluebell, Yellow Archangel, Wood Anemone, Moschatel, Early-purple Orchid and Ramsons (wood garlic). The Dormouse is present as are Roe and Muntjac deer. Scobb's Grove is a separate copse of damp Ash, Alder, Hazel and Willow woodland containing ferns, Small Teasel and the amazingly named Alternate- leaved-golden-saxifrage. There is also interesting bird life including owls.

Cleeve Common - the high point in so many ways

It's difficult to know where to begin when talking about the final section of today's walk. It is literally the high point. At 1,083 feet (330 metres), Cleeve Hill is the highest point of the Cotswold Way and the Cotswolds as a whole. It's famous for wonderful views over Cheltenham and its racecourse, the Vale of Evesham, the Malverns and as far as the Black Mountains in Wales and the Shropshire hills. To the east stretch the gently undulating slopes of the Cotswolds dipping towards the low vales of Oxfordshire. Other features to look out for are the Gloucestershire and Warwickshire Railway line (as it approaches the race course), a significant government building of 'national importance' to make out and a controversial high rise office block also feature. There is a topograph at the peak showing points of interest of the long views.

Note there are two trig points. At 317m (just over 1000ft) above sea level, the first you see is after the radio mast on the edge of the escarpment and is a great spot to survey the valley stretching out below. But this is not the highest spot on Cleeve Hill. There is a second trig point, beyond the radio masts, that is 13m higher and is officially the 'top of the Cotswolds' at 330 metres (1083 feet) above sea level. It's very easy to find from the Pylon's car park, but it doesn't offer much of a view.

Cleeve Common, which extends over 400 hectares (1000 acres), is of national importance for the quality of its landscape, geology, archaeology, nature conservation and scientific interest. It is the largest area of unimproved limestone grassland in Gloucestershire. Almost all of it is SSSI designated,

Happy Valley

which means it is overseen by Natural England. It also contains a wealth of archaeological interest, including three Scheduled Monuments. Here are just some of the key points that draw on the Cleeve Common Trust's excellent website:

Geology. The Common is typical of the Cotswolds described in Chapter 2 with an escarpment, hilltop and dip (gradual) slope. The scarp slope, on the front of the Common, is the most accessible, while the hilltop is wide open grassland used extensively for recreation (including the golf course). The dip slope at the back of the Common includes deep valleys such as Padcombe Bottom. This is often referred to as the 'wilderness area', rich in plant, insect and bird life and a place where you can enjoy a truly 'away from it all' feeling.

The bedrock of the upper reaches of the Common is oolitic limestone. However, the majority of the height of the Cotswold Escarpment is made up of Early Jurassic (liassic) clays and silts. Cleeve is the only area of the Cotswolds where the full sequence of 'Inferior' Oolite rocks can be seen. Two layers, the 'Phillipsiana' and the 'Bourguetia' beds, are unique to Cleeve Hill and not visible anywhere else in Britain.

One of the more unusual geological features of the Common is the presence at the surface of sands and sandstone of the 'Harford Member' (one of the types of limestone). In the 18th and 19th centuries, this fine sand was taken off by donkey for use in the Staffordshire potteries. At Rolling Bank Quarry, you will find an information board telling you about the underlying geology of Cleeve Hill. This was installed by the Gloucestershire Geology Trust, who have also produced an illustrated geology trail guide. Rolling Bank Quarry is situated near the top of the escarpment, along from the Golf Clubhouse and directly behind the 18th tee.

Quarrying. For centuries the limestone has been quarried for building. Different quarries give access to different layers of rock with varying uses. Smooth-grained blocks with few imperfections, such as Lower Freestone, made good building stone. Coarser, rubbly rocks containing many fossils, like 'Gryphite' or 'Trigonia Grit', were suitable for roads and field walls. These rocks are named after the main fossil found in them, 'Gryphaea' (or devil's toenail) and 'Trigonia', two distinctive species of 'bivalves'. As you'll see, quarrying for stone, gravel and sand in recent centuries has left striking but unnatural rock faces and disused workings, particularly along the front face of the hill and the valley sides further back.

Limestone grassland. Once upon a time, like most of Britain, Cleeve Common was covered with dense woodland. This was cleared starting from around 6000 years ago to make way for farming. The landscape you see today is therefore 'man-made' grassland. Most of Cleeve Common consists of 'unimproved limestone grassland', found on shallow, free-draining and alkaline soils. Unlike much of the surrounding land, this grassland has not been agriculturally improved - ploughed and re-seeded or treated with artificial fertiliser or herbicides. The only management over the centuries has been extensive grazing and some cutting back of scrub.

Limestone grassland is a harsh environment with thin soil, poor in nutrients and so all types of plants face a struggle to survive. This battle for survival makes room for great diversity – no single species can become dominant leading to a great variety of wildflowers and grasses. Thus, several types of grass can be found, including short turf of fescues and bents and taller tor-grass, upright brome and meadow oat-grass. In spring and summer lime-loving flowers are widespread, including bright yellow bird's foot trefoil, burnet-saxifrage, small scabious, horseshoe vetch, carline thistles and harebells. Several types of orchid are to be seen, too, particularly bee orchid, common spotted orchid, pyramidal orchid and the rarer musk orchid.

Although most of the Common is unimproved limestone grassland, unusually for the Cotswolds there is acidic soil in some areas where 'Harford Sands' outcrop at the surface giving rise to acid grassland and small patches of heath. Scrub of all different ages adds to the diversity and is vital for birds and reptiles. Scattered trees make good perches for hunting raptors and woodland areas around the edges of the Common support a completely different range of species. Running and standing water in the Washpool valley and several ponds provide yet another habitat for amphibians, freshwater invertebrates and aquatic plants and provides drinking and bathing opportunities for birds and mammals. Gorse and heather thrive where the soil is neutral or acidic, giving the Common a heathland feel. In areas where soils are acid you will see heather, tormentil, heath-grass, heath milkwort, heath bedstraw and several species of moss that are only found on acid soil. There are also stands of bracken in one corner of the Common beyond Nutterswood. In the marshy fringes of the Washpool are local flat-sedge, bristle club-rush and whorl-grass. In the marshy fringes of the Washpool are bristle club-rush, whorl-grass and the nationally vulnerable flat-sedge. There is an exceptional range of bryophytes (mosses and liverworts) on the Common including some national rarities. Click here for further information on the Common Commissioners' efforts to conserve these important species.

Perhaps not surprisingly, there isn't much woodland on the Common. Those few trees that adorn the skyline show the effects of exposure to the predominantly south-westerly winds. Notable are 'The Twins', an iconic pair of trees and the 'Single Beech', the highest tree in the Cotswolds at 317m. Even so, some thirty acres of new woodland has been planted at the far south-eastern extremity (West Down, going towards Charlton Abbots). This is named 'Wardens' Wood' in tribute to the Cotswold

Voluntary Wardens who undertook most of the planting. Elsewhere, there is scrubby growth in the lower part of Padcombe Bottom and a finger of woodland extending down Bentley Lane, towards Southam.

Wildlife. The range of habitats and diversity of the grassland across the Common makes it a fine home for many species. In spring and summer, lime-loving flowers are widespread, including bright yellow bird's-foot trefoil, wild thyme, common rock-rose, fairy flax, burnet-saxifrage, dropwort, milkwort, small scabious, carline thistles and harebells. The endangered purple milk-vetch is found in short turf on the Common and conservation efforts are underway to secure its range on the Common. Several types of orchid can be seen, particularly early purple orchid, bee orchid, common spotted orchid, pyramidal orchid and the rare frog and musk orchids. Many different grasses can be found, including quaking grass, short turf of fescues and bents and taller tor-grass, upright brome and meadow oat-grass. On the steep slopes of the Washpool Valley are rare plants associated with the thin and fragile scree, including red hemp-nettle and limestone fern. In some of the woodlands around the edges of the Common you can find bluebells, wood anemone, primroses and opposite-leaved golden saxifrage.

The Common has a tremendous variety of fungi and is particularly rich in colourful waxcap species which are found in the grasslands in summer and autumn. You might also see 'fairy rings' of fungi in the grass. These get bigger each year and can be seen even without the fruiting fungi due to the fungal mycelium in the soil beneath the ring affecting nutrient levels and grass growth.

With such a variety of habitats, it comes as no surprise that there is also a great diversity of invertebrate life on the Common. Butterflies such as the dark green fritillary, dingy skipper and common blue thrive on limestone grassland whilst the green hairstreak likes some scrub for shelter. Burnet moths with their vivid red and black colouring are easy to see during the day, and you might see the much rarer cistus forester, a metallic-green day-flying moth. There are snails to be found too, such as the heath snail 'Helicella itala', and spiders such as the 'funnel-web' 'Agelena labyrinthica' and, just off the Common, the very rare purseweb spider 'Atypus affinis'. A particularly notable find in the summer of 2010 was the small bug, 'Hallodapus montadoni', which had not been seen in Gloucestershire since 1944!

Bird life is plentiful on the Common. Skylarks nest on the ground in rough grass and can be heard singing in spring and early summer. Meadow pipits might look similar at first glance, but during their display flight they sing as they 'parachute' to the ground, whereas skylarks stay high up whilst singing continuously. Stonechat, linnet and yellowhammer can be seen all year round, perched conspicuously on gorse and scrub. Returning to the Common after wintering in warmer climes, willow warbler, blackcap, chiffchaff and cuckoo can be heard singing from scrub in spring and early summer. With luck, you might also see scarcer species like wheatear, redstart, whinchat and tree pipit. Most years, ring ouzels drop in for a week or two on their migration between their breeding grounds in northern England, Scotland or Scandinavia and their wintering grounds in the Atlas mountains of north Africa. In winter, watch out for large flocks of redwing and fieldfare feeding on hawthorn berries or perhaps with a bit of luck a short-eared owl.

Last, but not least, the Common is home to four species of reptile: adder, grass snake, common lizard and slow-worm - all of which are protected and their numbers monitored to help conserve their habitat. Many species of mammal also make the Common their home. There are rabbits in

The bee orchid

The common spotted orchid

The musk orchid

The pyramidal orchid

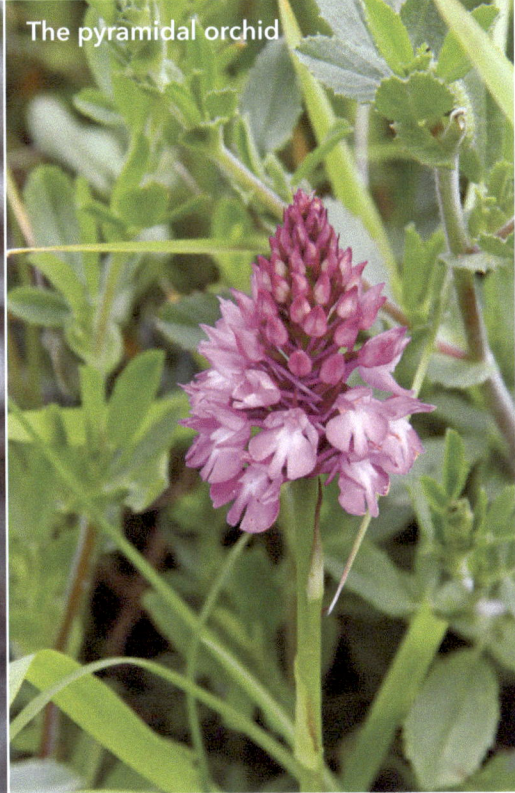

By kind permission of Jean Booth

abundance, especially in the sandy areas on the hilltop, and a few hares. Increasing numbers of deer forage in the fringes of the Common: most are roe deer or the small but noisy muntjac. Grey squirrels are abundant in the woodlands. There are four badger setts on the Common itself and two more a short distance away. You might also catch sight of the occasional fox, stoat, weasel, shrew or mole. Colonies of bats ('lesser horseshoe' and 'Myotis' species) inhabit some of the rock faces.

Archaeology and history. The Common abounds in archaeological prehistoric and Roman settlements including three 'Scheduled' sites. You can still see the shape of one of these, the Iron Age hill fort, above the small settlement of Nutterswood. One of the many hill forts spread along the Cotswold escarpment, it dates from around 500 BCE and was probably built initially as a single bank and ditch, with the second ring added some two centuries later. Like many castles that followed centuries later, it was probably a symbol of power and wealth as much as a defensive construction. Sitting on the edge of the escarpment, it would be visible for miles around and was perhaps the seat of a local chieftain. Much of the hillfort has been destroyed through quarrying in the last 300 years. Today it encloses some three acres and is approximately one third of a circle. It isn't known, though, whether it was once a complete circle or stopped along the original natural edge of the scarp.

There is also an ancient boundary in the form of a long, linear earthwork crossing the hill called the 'Cross Dyke'. Probably the oldest archaeological feature of the Common, the 'Cross Dyke' is a long ditch and bank earthwork originating in the Bronze Age (before 700 BCE) and so predating the iron-age hill fort. It runs from near the top of Rising Sun Lane diagonally up the escarpment (where it is popularly called 'The Staircase'), over the edge and then swings left into Dry Bottom and Postlip Quarries. Probably built as a territorial boundary, this linear earthwork suggests that even this long ago, dwellers in the vale at the foot of the scarp had staked their claim to a large part of the hilltop. Many centuries later, it became the manorial boundary between Southam and Cleeve. Today's parish boundary between Southam and Woodmancote still follows this historic line. The most visible sections are 'the Staircase' on the escarpment, about 300 metres up and right from the top of Rising Sun Lane, the section over the lip of the hill (between the Golf Course 15th green and the quarry area) and the diagonal run down the other side (above the 11th tee).

The third 'Scheduled' site is a circular earthwork known as 'The Ring'. It's on the upper part of the scarp slope and some 50 metres in diameter. It is believed to have been built as an enclosure for animals in the early centuries AD and provides evidence of the use of the Common as pasture in Roman-British times.

As well as the Commons' scheduled sites, there are other earthworks that provide clues to the past. At the foot of the cliff below 'The Twins' (the prominent pair of trees at the top of the escarpment), there is a square stone block known as 'Huddlestone's Table'. It's said that this marks the spot where King Kenulf of Mercia bade farewell to several important guests, including the king of Kent, after dedicating the great Benedictine Abbey in Winchcombe in 811. Although a fine spot for such a parting, it does not lie on tracks in use at that time and, in any case, the Huddlestone family did not move to Southam until the 1520's!

Built in 1897, the 'Washpool' or 'Sheep Wash' is a deep, keyhole-shaped trough with stone sides. It is a reminder of the importance of Cleeve Common to sheep farming in the past. Photographs from the 1920's and 1930's show temporary pens containing hundreds of sheep gathered for dipping.

They were herded into the round well and, once thoroughly soaked, allowed to scramble out up the narrow ramp (the fence is a recent addition for safety). The sheep wash was fed with water from the pool immediately above it, formed by damming the stream that flows down from a spring about 200 metres up the valley which is known, appropriately, as 'Watery Bottom'. Cleeve Common Trust undertook a renovation project of the area between 2018-2020.

On the hilltop part of the Common, near the radio masts, is a historic watering hole or dewpond, which was restored in 2000 as an experiment in a traditional way of providing drinking water for grazing stock. The pond is some 20 metres across and two metres deep (although the maximum water depth is only about one metre). It collects rainwater and run-off from the surrounding land. Traditionally, a lining of clay prevented the water from soaking away, but in this modern restoration a butylene sheet liner is used instead. The dewpond has provided a source of water not only for sheep, but also for wildlife on the Hill and is visited by a wide range of birds. Cattle have been kept out for fear of damaging the lining. So far, it has never dried up, even in hot summers.

Recreation. In case you're wondering, the first golf course on the Common opened in 1891 and its clubhouse dates from 1895. It reflects the fact that the Common has always played an important part in the recreational life of the local community. You might not think it likely, but once upon a time the Common was also home to Cheltenham racecourse. It was during Cheltenham's boom time growth as a fashionable spa resort in the 19th century. Horse racing and training began in 1818 and lasted until 1855, when they moved to their current home at Prestbury Park - largely due, the Jockey Club explains, to the preachings of Cheltenham's Reverend Francis Close, leading to the disruption of meetings and the burning of the grandstand! There was a figure-of-eight race track and grandstand close to where the radio masts are today.

Maybe the move had something to do with concerns about gambling. The Commissioners remind us that the Bylaws include many references to leisure activities, some quaint by today's standards, such as the prohibition on 'gambling, betting, or playing with cards or dice at any time on the Common'.

Management of the Common. Important though the natural features of the Common are, it's ownership and management also deserve our attention. Contrary to what you might think, 'commons' do not necessarily belong to the public. Strictly speaking, Cleeve Common is privately owned by the descendants of the Lords of the Manor of Southam and Bishops Cleeve. Visitors have the right to roam on foot here and certain local landowners have grazing (or 'commoners') rights, entitling them to graze specified numbers of sheep, cattle and other animals between April and November. Cleeve Common is also different to many other commons in that it is managed by a group of 'Conservators' in a charitable Trust. The 'Conservators' were established in 1890 by an Act of Parliament, which gave them sole management responsibility for Cleeve Common, allowing them to make Bylaws to protect and preserve the site for generations to come. Today's Trustees are representatives appointed by local boroughs and parishes and the landowner.

In the upkeep of the Common, the trustees have a couple of groups of very able assistants whom they affectionately describe as 'lawn mowers on four legs'. Historically, overgrazing by one of these, the sheep, was a problem, helping to explain the need for the regulation of grazing rights. Recently by contrast, a decline in stock farming means undergrazing is now the biggest threat to the survival of this wildflower-rich grassland. Without grazing (aided by human conservation), coarse grasses, gorse and hawthorn scrub would take over. These would out-compete the wild flowers, some of which are critically endangered nationally, greatly reducing the wildlife diversity and the value of the Common for recreation.

Sheep are good for grazing over a wide area, especially the slopes and shorter grass. There are typically up to 1500 sheep on the Common at the height of the grazing season. However, you probably don't know that sheep are pretty canny selective grazers, favouring sweet, lush grass and flowers first. They graze with a mowing effect, nibbling the grass off close to the ground layer. This is where the cattle you'll find on the Common come in. Cattle are needed to tackle the taller and coarser grassland and to introduce variation in the structure of the grassland sward. Apparently, they wrap their long tongues around tall, rough grass and pull; they also are much less fussy and graze even the steepest of banks. Also, due to their size, some beasts weighing close to one tonne, they are very good at trampling the scrub that the Commissioners are trying to manage. Their weight helps break up gorse and thorn, slowing regeneration of this scrub.

Meet the Galloway - steam roller and lawn mower!

Cattle were reintroduced to the Common in 1993 for the summer months, following many years of under-grazing. Meeting Natural England's targets, it was agreed, called for year-round grazing. Therefore in 2006 the Board of Conservators took the major step of purchasing its own herd of black and belted Galloways. They are perfect for over-wintering on the Common; in fact this breed actively dislikes being shut indoors. They are just right for a public place such as Cleeve Common as by nature they are placid – and do not have intimidating horns! During the winter months, the Galloway cattle are contained in large temporary paddocks in order to focus the grazing on the areas that most need it. In summer, they roam freely over the whole Common, along with the sheep.

Cotswold Way Circular Walk

It must be pretty clear that Cleeve Common has a great deal to offer. Trying to fit everything in on a walk that you started in Seven Springs is likely to lead to frustration. You should think, therefore, about returning for a full day's outing. You could, for example, make the Cotswold Way Circular Walk No 5 - 'The Cleeve Hill Ring' - the basis of a tour that incorporates two trails that the Cleeve Common Commissioners have made available: one deals with historical matters and the other geological,

In the words of the National Trails website presenting the 'Cleeve Hill Ring':

'This breathtaking walk leads you over open hilltops, across streams and through woodlands, immersing you in one of the country's most fascinating and precious habitats – limestone grassland. Over half of this wildflower and butterfly rich natural resource is within the Cotswolds and some of the finest examples are on Cleeve Common. The unsurpassed views along this route therefore, are the perfect backdrop for getting even closer to the outstanding natural beauty of the Cotswold Way.

- Distance: 6 miles (Shorter route 4 miles). Duration: 3½ – 4½ hrs (Shorter: 2 – 3 hrs). Difficulty: Moderate, no stiles but some steep sections (Shorter: Easy, no stiles and mostly level)'.
- You can download the map from www.nationaltrail.co.uk

Car Parking

- For the start from Seven Springs, see the end point on the previous stage.
- You can park on Cleeve Common just past the Cleeve Hill Golf Club - it's shown on the OS Map and the nearest postcode is (GL52 3PW). Alternatively, you can go on to Winchcombe and usually find space in the Back Lane long stay car park (GL54 5PZ).

Chapter 11
Time for a history lesson
From Cleeve Common to Hayles Fruit Farm

If the previous stage was about nature, the focus of this one is mainly on English history. You have a famous Neolithic burial barrow to visit, followed by a Roman villa. You walk through the Anglo-Saxon town that was once a royal seat of Mercia's kings. One of these was Offa, no less, who built the dyke between England and Wales bearing his name. Not so well known is that it was Offa who helped to lay the foundations of a unified England for Alfred the Great to build on. The middle ages are strongly represented too. You will have an opportunity to visit a castle where the last of Henry VIII's six queens is buried. You will also pass one of the churches that features in the list of famous Cotswold 'wool' churches, although it probably shouldn't. It does, however, have famous gargoyles - one figure is said to be the model for the Mad Hatter in Lewis Carroll's *Alice in Wonderland*. Finally, you will pass the splendid remains of a famous Cistercian abbey, which has its own recently restored railway halt.

From Cleeve Common to Belas Knap

From the car park at the golf club on the B4632, you drop down to Postlip Hall. There's been a house here since before the Norman Conquest, but the Chapel, built about 1145, is the oldest of the present buildings. A Grade 1 listed medieval Hall House, probably dating from the fifteenth century, is hiding inside the NE corner. Giles Broadway, said to be an entrepreneur and 'chancer', added the much grander Jacobean frontage in 1614. The rest of the house was added gradually thereafter around a central courtyard. The Tithe Barn's origins are a bit of a mystery, as no documents have survived. It might be as old as the 12C Chapel or could have been built at any point between 1140 and about 1400.

In the early 1970s, Postlip Hall was taken over by the Postlip Housing Association and divided into eight separate units, each with its own front door (and usually a back door) so everybody has a private 'house' that's part of a much bigger cooperative framework. People can thus move fairly freely between private life and group life. They share some communal rooms and also the fifteen-acre grounds, pond, stream and kitchen garden. They don't cook communally, but eat informally together every now & then, especially in the summer.

Not far from the trail on your left is

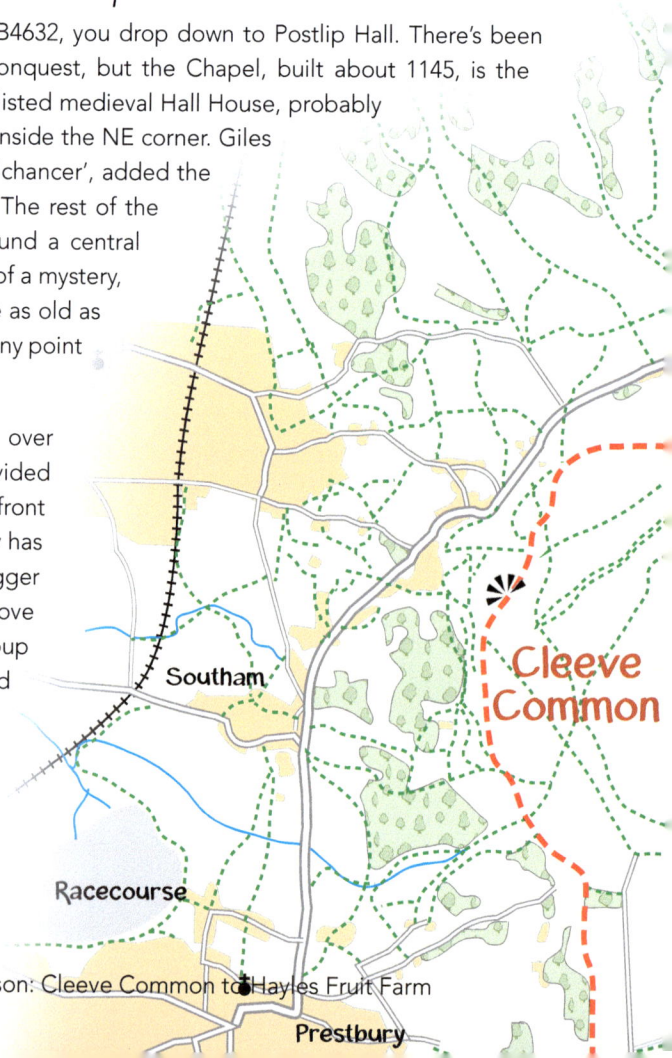

Southam

Racecourse

Cleeve Common

Prestbury

N

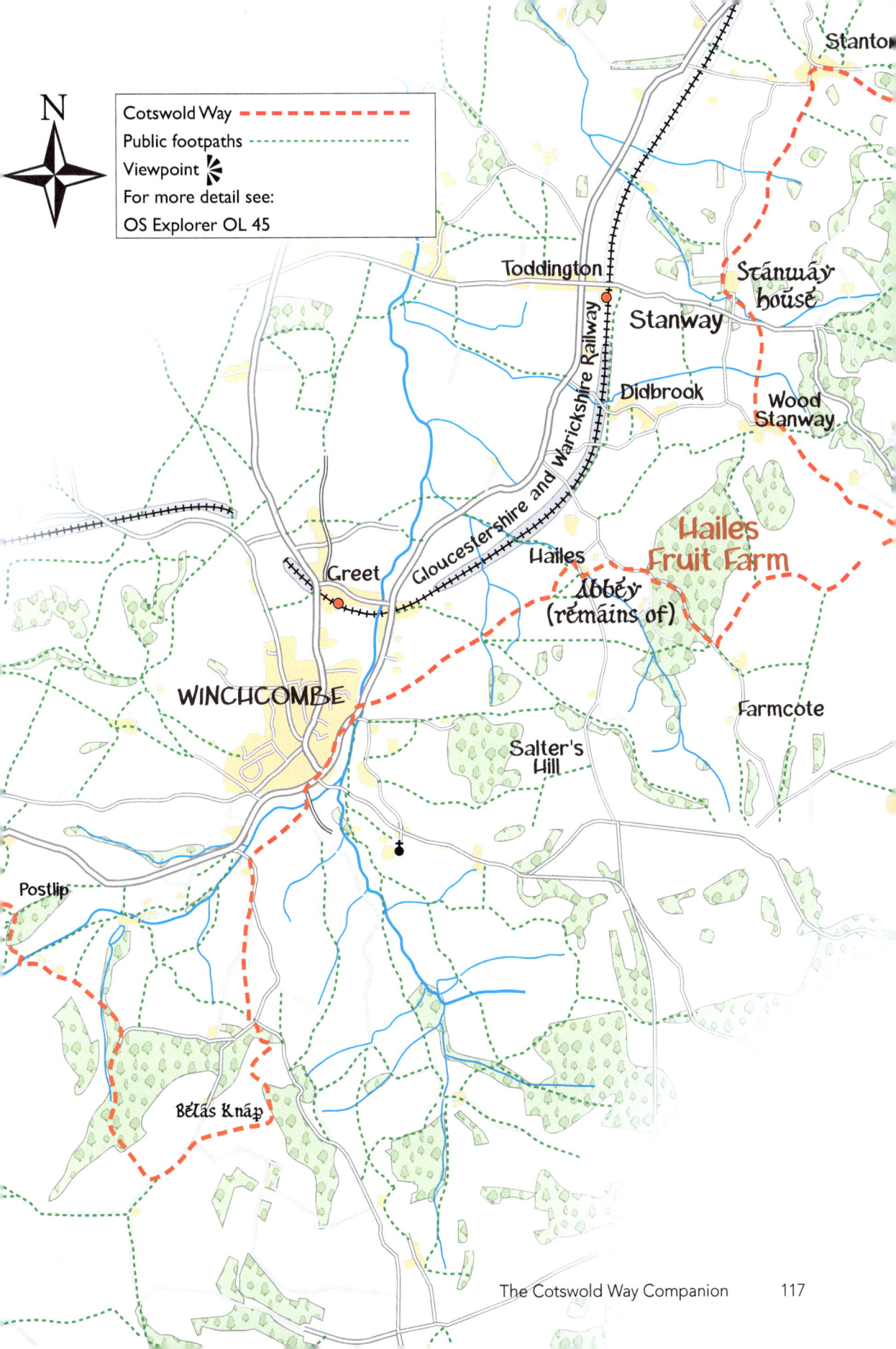

Stanton

Toddington

Stanway house

Stanway

Gloucestershire and Warickshire Railway

Didbrook

Wood Stanway

Greet

Hailes

Hailes Fruit Farm

Abbey (remains of)

WINCHCOMBE

Salter's Hill

Farmcote

Postlip

Belas Knap

Postlip Mill. This was first recorded as milling flour around 1066, using a large water wheel. Since 1733, however, paper has been manufactured at Postlip Mill. Today it makes specialist filter paper.

Next up is Belas Knap, which is a neolithic, chambered long barrow. It's reckoned to be about 5,000 years old and a scheduled ancient monument in the care of English Heritage, but managed by Gloucestershire County Council. Its name is probably a combination of Latin and Old English. 'Belas' is likely to be derived from the Latin word for 'beautiful', ('bello' in Italian today), which could describe the hill or its view. 'Knap' is derived from the Old English for the top, crest, or summit of a hill.

Belas Knap is described in the Historic England designation listing statement as an 'outstanding example representing a group of long barrows commonly referred to as the 'Cotswold-Severn group', named after the region in which they occur'. Altogether within the 'Cotswolds-Severn' area, there are reckoned to be around 200 known long barrows with some to be found within the Cotswolds. These long burrows, it seems, appeared in the region fairly abruptly around 3700 BCE, the tradition of their building probably spreading north along the Atlantic coast as the 'Explainer' in Chapter 2 described. They continued to be built for about 600 years. By 2600 BCE, however, very few of them had chambers that remained in use and many had been deliberately blocked up.

A particular feature is that these long burrows have a similar oval or trapezoid shape. In not so plain English, this means it's a quadrilateral with at least one pair of parallel sides, which may be vertical, horizontal or slanting …

Belas Knap is reckoned to be some 70 metres from north-south, 26 metres wide at the northern end,

Belas Knap

Belas Knap

17 metres wide at the southern end and has a maximum height of around three metres. The mound is flanked on each side by a ditch from which material was quarried during the construction of the monument. These have become infilled over the years, but survive as buried features around five metres wide. There is a Bronze Age 'bowl' barrow 80 metres to the south-west of the long barrow and the two monuments are intervisible.

Belas Knap's seemingly impressive entrance, which consists of two standing stones and a lintel stone, is in fact 'false'. The burial chambers are entered from the sides of the barrow - when closed and covered by earth they would have been invisible from the outside.

The actual burial chambers are down the long East and West sides of the barrow and at its Southern foot. There are four such chambers, two on opposite sides near the middle, one at the South-East angle and one at the South end. These are formed of upright stone slabs, linked by dry-stone walling and originally had corbelled (i.e. simple vaulted) roofs.

In the 1863-1865 excavations, the skeletal remains of five children, aged between 6 months and 8 years, were found among the rubble blocking the 'false entrance', along with the skull of a young adult male, horse and pig bones and fragments of pottery and serrated flint blade. Excavations in 1963 found the remains of 38 human skeletons, together with animal bones, flint implements and pottery of the end of the Neolithic period, around 2000 BC. These burials, however, occurred over a long period of time and it may be that none date to the time when the mound was built.

Not long after Belas Knap, you can make a slight detour from the trail onto the Winchcombe Way to Wadfield Farm, where you'll find the site of a large courtyard Roman villa first discovered during ploughing in 1863. According to 'Historic England Research Records' on Heritage Gateway, the Roman Villa lies on a narrow natural shelf on an east facing slope. The building, it seems, was in several phases. Excavations have revealed almost the whole ground plan of a courtyard villa, including the remains beyond of massive but irregular walls and a roughly paved courtyard. It looks as if there were three wings around a court with a bath suite in the south range, living accommodation on the west range and rooms of uncertain function on the north range.

The small finds preserved at Sudeley Castle included coins of Domitian and Arcadius, along with coarse pottery and possible small fragments of Samian Ware. Brooches were also found, including one of Fan-tail type, and a ring with an intaglio and the foot of a statue. A tessellated pavement, in perfect condition, found at that time was also removed to Sudeley Castle, but not before a large portion of it had been robbed. A stone building, now damaged, has been erected over the mosaic floor, which is also deteriorating.

More recently, Heritage Gateway reported investigations by the Gloucester and District Archaeological Research Group during the laying of the natural Gas pipeline had revealed a hitherto unknown Roman building situated south of the Wadfield villa (at SP 023260). It measured nine metres by twelve. Shallow rubbish pits were found to the west of it, the many potsherds discovered further up the hillside thought to indicate the possibility of more buildings near the road. A skeleton was unearthed by the pipeline contractors above Wadfield (at SP 022260), along with pottery associated with the burial deposit.

Anglo-Saxon Winchcombe - King Offa and the Mercians

After coming down the hill from Belas Knap, the trail takes you through the town of Winchcombe. Though small in absolute terms, Winchcombe is one of the largest communities on the Cotswold Way. Indeed, along with Dursley and Wotton-under-Edge, it is just one of the three towns whose population is above 5,000.

Winchcombe has two main claims to fame today. The first is to be the landing point of one of the largest meteorites to have hit the UK - it was observed entering the Earth's atmosphere as a fluorescent green fireball at 21:54 hours on 28 February 2021. As Wikipedia tells us, it's around 4.6 billion-year-old and originates from the asteroid belt between Mars and Jupiter. If you'd like to know more about the meteorite's origins, unexpected arrival and scientific significance, make sure to visit the display in the Winchcombe Museum in the High Street.

Winchcombe's other claim to fame is to be the 'Walkers' capital of the Cotswolds. It certainly has a strong case. It was one of the first Walkers are Welcome towns in the country and, along with Dursley and Wotton-under-edge, one of three along the national trail route. As Chapter 2 has already pointed out, it's at the epicentre of several long distance footpaths including the Winchcombe Way, the Wardens' Way, the Gloucestershire Way, the Isbourne Way and the Windrush Way. A host of local walks are also to be found on the Winchcombe Welcomes Walkers website.

As the 'Heritage Centre' at Winchcombe's Museum confirms, however, it's the town's illustrious history that perhaps most deserves your attention on this stage of the walk. Winchcombe was especially prominent in Anglo-Saxon times. By the early eighth century, the place had become, for reasons that aren't entirely clear, a major royal centre of a people known as the 'Hwicce'. The boundaries of the kingdom are uncertain, but it's likely that they coincided with those of the old Diocese of Worcester. 'Hwicce' survives in Worcestershire in the names of Wichenford and Wychbury Hill, in Whichford in Warwickshire and in Wychwood in Oxfordshire. In addition, the local government district of Wychavon owes the first element of its name to the old kingdom. Likely, too, is that the ruling dynasty of the 'Hwicce' sprang from intermarriage between Anglian and Romano- British leading families.

This might not seem to amount to much, but by the 7th century AD the territory had been absorbed into the kingdom of Mercia. For some two hundred years, between c.626 and c.825, the kingdom of Mercia was the dominant force among the seven Anglo-Saxon Kingdoms known as the 'heptarchy'. Historians such as Sir Frank Stenton talk about the 'Mercian Supremacy'. Along with Penda, an earlier king of Mercia, Offa, who ruled 757–796, is a major figure. Understandably, he's come to be associated with the famous dyke named after him. Much more importantly, however, it was Offa who effectively achieved the unification of England south of the Humber estuary and so laid the foundations for Alfred to build on some hundred years later.

As for Winchcombe itself, Offa is said to have founded a nunnery here in 790. A few years later, in 798, either he or his successor but one, Cenwulf, began to build a great monastery there on the grounds to the east end of today's St Peter's Church. Apparently, it was dedicated in 811 with much splendour by Wulfred, Archbishop of Canterbury, in the presence of the kings of East Anglia and Kent, thirteen bishops, ten ealdormen, and a great concourse of people.

The country of 'Winchcombshire' was also created in 1007 during the reign of Ethelred the Unready. Frequent Danish incursions into the west of England made strengthening local administration - and tax gathering - an urgent priority. Five counties were formed - Winchcombeshire joining Gloucestershire, Worcestershire, Warwickshire and Oxfordshire. Winchcombeshire didn't survive the decade, however, being disbanded by Eardric Streona, who was Ealdorman of Mercia. You'll find further details in Julian Whybra's 1990 book in the *Studies in Anglo-Saxon History* series, entitled 'A Lost English County: Winchcombeshire in the Tenth and Eleventh Centuries'.

Eardic has another claim to fame or, rather, infamy. According to Wikipedia, in 2005, he was selected by *BBC's History Magazine* as the 11th century's worst Briton on account of his dishonesty and flip flopping between the Anglo-Saxon and Danish contenders for the throne. It didn't do him much good. Canute had him killed in 1017.

Especially important in making Winchcombe Abbey very rich as well as famous was the presence of St. Kenelm's tomb. As Chapter 2 has already explained, the legends associated with Kenelm meant that pilgrims flocked to Winchcombe throughout the early middle ages.

As well as springs sprouting up from the ground in various places, Kenelm's soul supposedly rose in the form of a dove and flew to Rome carrying a scroll which it dropped at the feet of the Pope with the news of his death. The message on the scroll read: 'Low in a mead of kine under a thorn, of head bereft, lieth poor Kenelm king-born'.

When at the end of the fifteenth century, Abbot Richard Kidderminster began to write the history of the monastery, he could not gather any certain information as to the endowment provided by Cenwulf. He believed, nonetheless, that it consisted of lands at Sherborne, Bledington, Enstone, Honeybourne, Adelmington, Alne, Twyning, Charlton Abbots, Stanton, Snowshill, and Newton. In its heyday, Winchcombe Abbey owned 25,300 acres (102 kms²) in 13 parishes. Snowshill Manor was owned by Winchcombe Abbey from 821 until the Dissolution of the Monasteries in 1539, when its buildings were given to Lord Seymour of Sudeley who carried out the demolition.

Although there is not much left of Anglo-Saxon Winchcombe, parts of the ramparts from that era are preserved as earthwork in the land on the southern side of Back Lane. Some of the stones from the demolished Winchcombe Abbey can also still be found around the town.

Medieval Winchcombe - a 'wool church' and a castle

As Chapter 2 pointed out, St Peter's Church in Winchcombe is usually regarded as one of the great 'wool' churches in the Cotswolds. Strictly speaking, however, according to Britain Express, the first written record of a church dedicated to St Peter in Winchcombe comes from 1175, when a church associated with the Benedictine Abbey here is mentioned.

St Peter's, Winchcombe

Winchcombe

That Norman church gradually fell into disrepair and, in 1458, Abbot William began building its replacement. Also, rather than wool merchants, it was the lord of Sudeley Castle, Lord Ralph Boteler, who came up with most of the money to help finish the construction, the new church being completed in just ten years. It's reckoned to be an excellent example of late 15th century perpendicular style, with a high, wide nave and large clerestory windows filling the interior with light.

You'll see that the exterior of St Peter's is dominated by a striking west tower, 90 feet or 27.4 metres high, with eight pinnacles. If you're like most visitors, however, it might not be what you're looking for. Rather the main attraction is the carvings that embellish the battlemented roofline of the exterior. Often called gargoyles, they are technically 'grotesques' - if you don't know your 'gargoyles" from your 'grotesques', the former have water spouts passing through them and the latter don't. There are forty of these carvings; about twenty depict demonic creatures, and the remainder appear to be caricatures of locally important people, both civic figures and Abbey officials.

Especially famous, and said to be beloved of photographers, is a figure to the east of the porch who has a squat hat and seems to sit there grimacing. This is thought to be the model for the Mad Hatter in Lewis Carroll's *Alice in Wonderland*.

If you walk around the west end of the church, towards the west tower door, you will also see what appear to be pockmarks in the masonry of the north aisle wall. These are holes made by musket balls in the Civil War and tell a sad tale. As explained below, Sudeley castle was owned by the Chandos family who sided with King Charles. When Parliamentary troops took the town in 1643, they executed Royalist soldiers by firing squad, standing them up against the church wall.

Sudeley Castle

Sudeley Castle - home to one of Henry V111's Queens

Just to your right as the Cotswold Way comes into Winchcombe, you'll catch a glimpse of Sudeley Castle. To get a closer takes just a few minutes down the aptly named Castle Street. Grade I listed, the castle is set within a 1,200-acre estate and has ten notable gardens covering some 15 acres.

The Sudeley Castle website has a detailed timeline of its history. Although the origins of 'Sudeley' are lost, its name is said to be a corruption of the Anglo-Saxon Sudeleagh, meaning 'south lying pasture or clearing in forest'. Sudeley can most likely thank its early rise as a royal estate to its close proximity to Winchcombe and its royal patronage.

By the turn of the 11th century, Sudeley had grown into a manor house set in a Royal deer park, given as an extravagant gift from King Æthelred the Unready to his daughter Princess Goda of England on her wedding day. Despite William the Conqueror's policy of depriving Saxon nobles of their estates after the Norman Conquest of 1066, the family managed to retain Sudeley, Princess Goda's descendants holding Sudeley for another four centuries. Most probably, it took the form of a fortified manor house as mentioned in Chapter 2.

The building of a castle began in 1443 and is attributed to Ralph Boteler. He was the Lord High Treasurer of England at the time. The wherewithal, it seems, came from the spoils from the 100 years war with France. Later, Sudeley was seized by the crown and became the property of King Edward IV and King Richard III, who built its banqueting hall.

Most importantly, Sudeley became the home and final resting place of King Henry VIII's sixth wife, Catherine Parr. Catherine, who remarried Lord Seymour after the king's death, died at Sudeley on 5 September 1548 from what was described as 'childbed fever' - it was just five days after giving birth to her daughter Mary Seymour. It is said that, at the funeral, Lady Jane Grey was the chief mourner and the ecclesiastical reformer Myles Coverdale preached his first Protestant sermon. Catherine Parr's burial in the castle's church makes Sudeley the only privately owned castle in the world to have a Queen of England buried in its grounds. Subsequently, Sudeley became the home of the Chandos family. Queen Elizabeth I, it seems, was a frequent visitor and is said to have held a three-day party there to celebrate the defeat of the Spanish Armada.

A half century later, unfortunately for the castle, the Chandos family supported the King during the English Civil War. Charles I stayed at Sudeley and Prince Rupert used the castle as a military base. Consequently, in 1649, parliamentary forces laid siege to it and, after the end of the war, parliament ordered its 'slighting' (demolition) to ensure that it could never again be used as a military post. Apparently, the process took some five months to complete and largely dismantled the inner courtyard and royal apartment rooms, but strangely left much of the outer courtyard intact.

Sudeley remained largely in ruins for nearly two hundred years. It was only in 1837 that the castle found salvation, being rescued by the wealthy Worcester glove-makers, brothers John and William Dent. They turned the castle into a family home and began an ambitious restoration programme. Their nephew, John Coucher Dent carried it on, when he inherited the Castle in 1855, his wife, Emma Brocklehurst, throwing herself enthusiastically into the work.

Today, Sudeley is the home of Lady Ashcombe and the Dent-Brocklehursts. The family continue to be committed to the continued preservation of the Castle and its treasures, along with the ongoing restoration and regeneration of the gardens,

Hailes Abbey and Hailes Church

Leaving Winchcombe on the road to Broadway, the national trail follows the course of the River Isbourne for a short stretch before turning right onto Puck Pit Lane - which was the original pilgrims' route from Winchcombe to our next destination. You'll come to it after about 1.5 miles. It's Hailes Abbey. According to the Wikipedia entry, it was founded by Richard Earl of Cornwall (the brother of Henry III) in 1246 with the help of Cistercian monks from Beaulieu in Hampshire. It seems that it was in grateful thanks for him surviving a shipwreck. Apparently, the construction of the abbey took some five years to complete and was consecrated in 1251. Henry 111, Queen Eleanor of Provence and 13 bishops attended the consecration ceremony.

English Heritage, who run the site on behalf of the Natural Trust, tells us about Hailes Abbey's renowned relic, 'the Holy Blood of Hailes'. This, allegedly, was a phial of Christ's own blood. It seems that Edmund, the son of Richard Earl of Cornwall, obtained the file while in Germany in 1268 - it was thought to have come from the coronation regalia of Charlemagne, the first Holy Roman Emperor. To the medieval mind, there could not have been a better provenance, and the relic was widely accepted as authentic.

The Holy Blood was held within a crystal container. A 16th-century seal, used to grant admission to the abbey's confraternity (or brotherhood), gives us the best impression of what the relic would have looked like. A priest is depicted holding an orb with a cross on top, which contains the Holy Blood of Hailes. You can view the object in 3D on the English Heritage website.

After dissolution, the Abbey's ownership was granted to Catherine Parr and passed down through her family. By the end of the 18th century, however, there had been extensive destruction leaving just

Hailes Abbey

a few of the cloister arches, together with the foundations as you will find them more or less today. The Abbey is now owned by the National Trust, but managed by English Heritage and you can visit for an entry charge.

In front of the Abbey remains, you will find a small church. According to Britain Express, 'if the exterior of Hailes church is unassuming, the interior is a marvel, a glimpse back in time'. As you enter, you see directly opposite you on the north wall, a very large painted figure of St Christopher, bearing the Christ child. St Christopher was the patron saint of travellers and his likeness is almost always found opposite the entrance, where people entering or leaving the church will see him. This is perhaps the most faded and indistinct of the Hailes wall paintings, says Britain Express, but better awaits. On the south wall, facing St Christopher across the nave, is a wonderful scene of a huntsman and three hounds chasing a hare. The figures are so full of life and vitality they seem like they will jump off the wall at any moment.

There's an interesting story that lies behind the positioning of the Abbey and the church. At first sight, it might not seem surprising - the church was there to serve as a chapel to the abbey. Indeed, it was so used for nearly four hundred years until the Abbey's dissolution. But things aren't quite so simple. The trouble with the obvious is that the church was consecrated in 1175 and so is nearly eighty years older than the abbey!

The church, it seems, was originally built to service the small village community that had grown up in and around the immediate vicinity. The incoming Cistercian monks, however, were well known for their preference for settling in remote areas and would appear to have objected to being exposed to such close worldly influence. A decision was therefore taken that has all the hallmarks of the advice that Sir Humphrey might have given in the Yes, Prime Minister long-running TV comedy series: it would be very difficult, both practically and politically, to move the church and much easier to shift the people. And so it came to pass: the church stayed and the Hailes villagers were moved to nearby Didbrook, which you'll see from the OS map is a mile or so to the north.

Something else you probably didn't know is that you can get to and from Hailes by train. Well, more or less. Thanks to funding from the Cotswold Conservation Board, the Gloucestershire Warwickshire Steam Railway (GWSR), the volunteer-run heritage railway, has recently completed the re-construction of a railway halt at Hailes Abbey. Just to confuse you, the halt isn't called 'Hailes', however, but 'Hayles' as in the name of the Fruit Farm just up the trail; it's also some 600 metres from the abbey in the other direction. For some reason, the halt was so named in Great Western Railway times, when there'd been a double-track line between Honeybourne and Cheltenham and the halt served by six daily rail services until closure in 1960. Although there isn't car parking at the reconstructed halt, GWSR suggests it's an ideal starting or finishing point for walkers or cyclists who want to make the round trip from Winchcombe or Toddington - trains can carry a limited number of bicycles. Charmingly, GWSR goes on to add the following instructions for would-be passengers:

Please note: Passengers wishing to join the train at the station will need to face the oncoming train and extend their arm horizontally to signal to the driver to stop the train. Those wishing to board at another station and alight at Hayles Abbey Halt will need to inform the guard when they join the train. Passengers need to be in one of the front two carriages to alight.

If you visit the halt, you might like to know it resembles the original timber-built structure, with cast-iron GWR notices, a corrugated-iron waiting shelter and traditional post-and-rail fencing.

Cotswold Way Circular Walk

Very appropriately, Winchcombe is the location of one of the twelve Cotswold Way Circular Walks. It's No 4 and named as 'Winchcombe and Belas Knap'. In the words of the National Trails website:

'This scenic and interesting little walk takes you from the delightfully unspoilt town of Winchcombe, along Cotswold Way routes old and new, and up to one of the area's most intriguing ancient

---

monuments, Belas Knap Long Barrow – A combination of history and scenery that will leave you eager to discover more of the National Trail and the inspirational landscape through which it runs.

- Distance: 5¼ miles (Short cut route 3½ miles). Duration: 3 – 4 hrs (Short cut 2 – 3 hrs). Difficulty: Moderate, some steep sections and stiles'.
- You can download the map from www.nationaltrail.co.uk

Car Parking

- For the start from Cleeve or Winchcombe, see the end point on the previous stage.
- You should be able to park at Hayles Fruit Farm (GL54 5PB) for a fee redeemable in the shop - currently £2.50. If not, try Salter's Lane in Hailes. Also there are sometimes spaces by Hailes Church opposite the abbey ruins (same postcode).

Chapter 12
A finish to relish
From Hayles Fruit Farm to Chipping Campden

It's difficult to imagine a better end to your walk - indeed, any walk - than the one you're about to experience. For this stage surely has everything you could ever want. You have ups and downs to remind you that walking the Cotswold Way is more than a matter of an afternoon stroll; wonderful views including some to the Malverns and the Clee and Clent Hills; a Jacobean manor with a working water mill, the highest gravity fountain in the world and a cricket pitch with connections to Peter Pan; perhaps the quintessential Cotswold village; the so-called 'jewel of the Cotswolds' famous for its tower and nuclear bunker; and a hill with Olympic ambitions as well as gorgeous views. You also end in what Pevsner, the famous architectural historian, describes as 'one of the best High Streets in the country' - and he should know because of his monumental 46-volume *The Buildings of England* series of county-by-county guides. There's also one of the Cotswolds' famous 'wool churches' as a bonus. If that's not enough, this stage is also home to three of the twelve Cotswold Way Circular Walks for you to return to sometime.

From Hayles Fruit Farm to Stumps Cross

You start from Hayles Fruit Farm, which is one of a number that Lord Sudeley had planted at the end of the 19th century, with a climb in the first mile passing Hailes Wood on your left and the Iron Age fort of Beckbury Camp on your right. Pause there for a moment and look down the avenue of trees to Stanway House and, if you're lucky, you might see the fountain, more about which later.

On to Stumps Cross, where it's confusing because there isn't a cross - just a stump and small monument that's been recently restored. Regrettably, nothing seems to be known about the monument - there is no inscription other than graffiti, though the tall niche would appear to have held a figure and so, perhaps, there's some association with Hailes Abbey. More positively, if

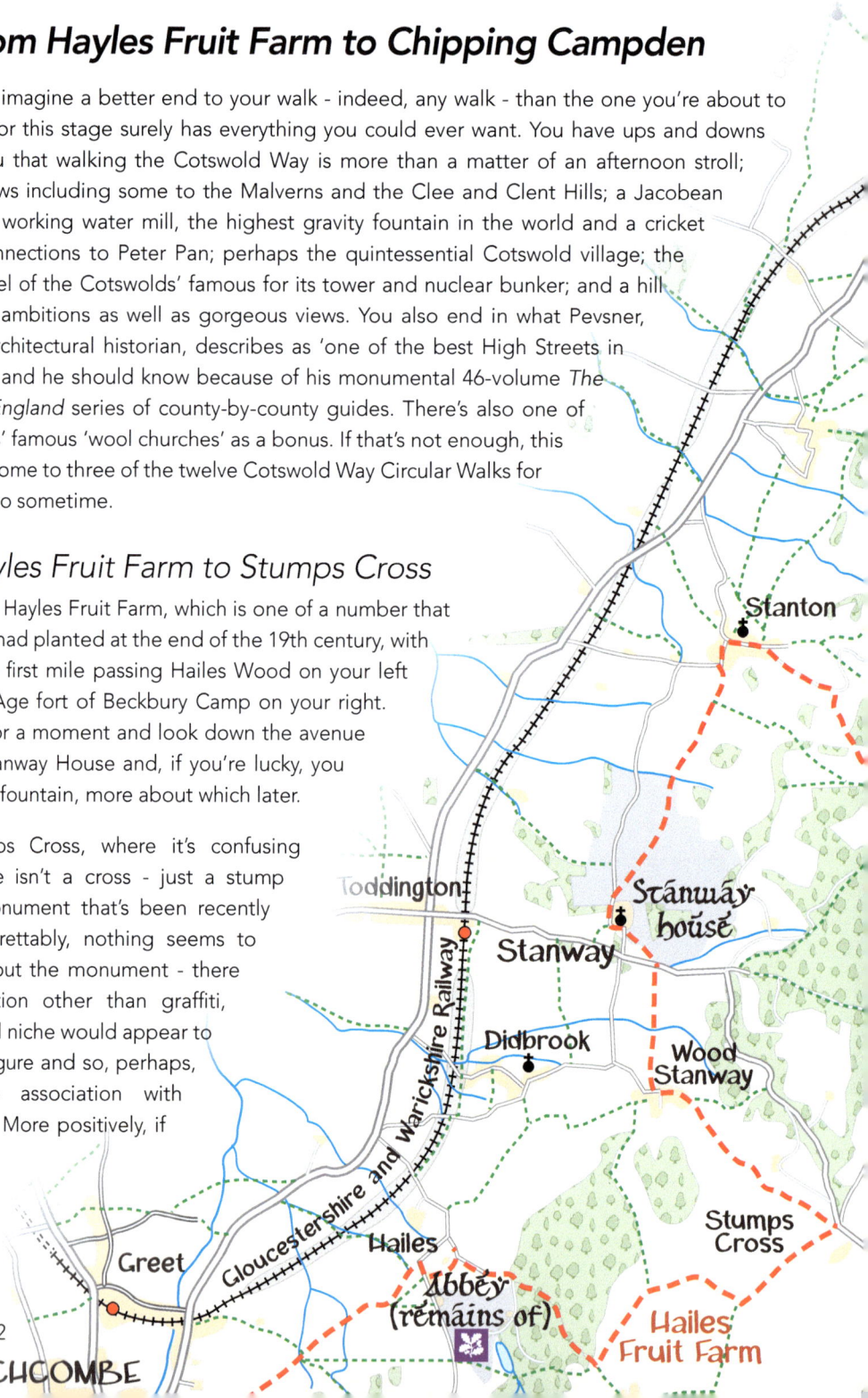

Map Legend

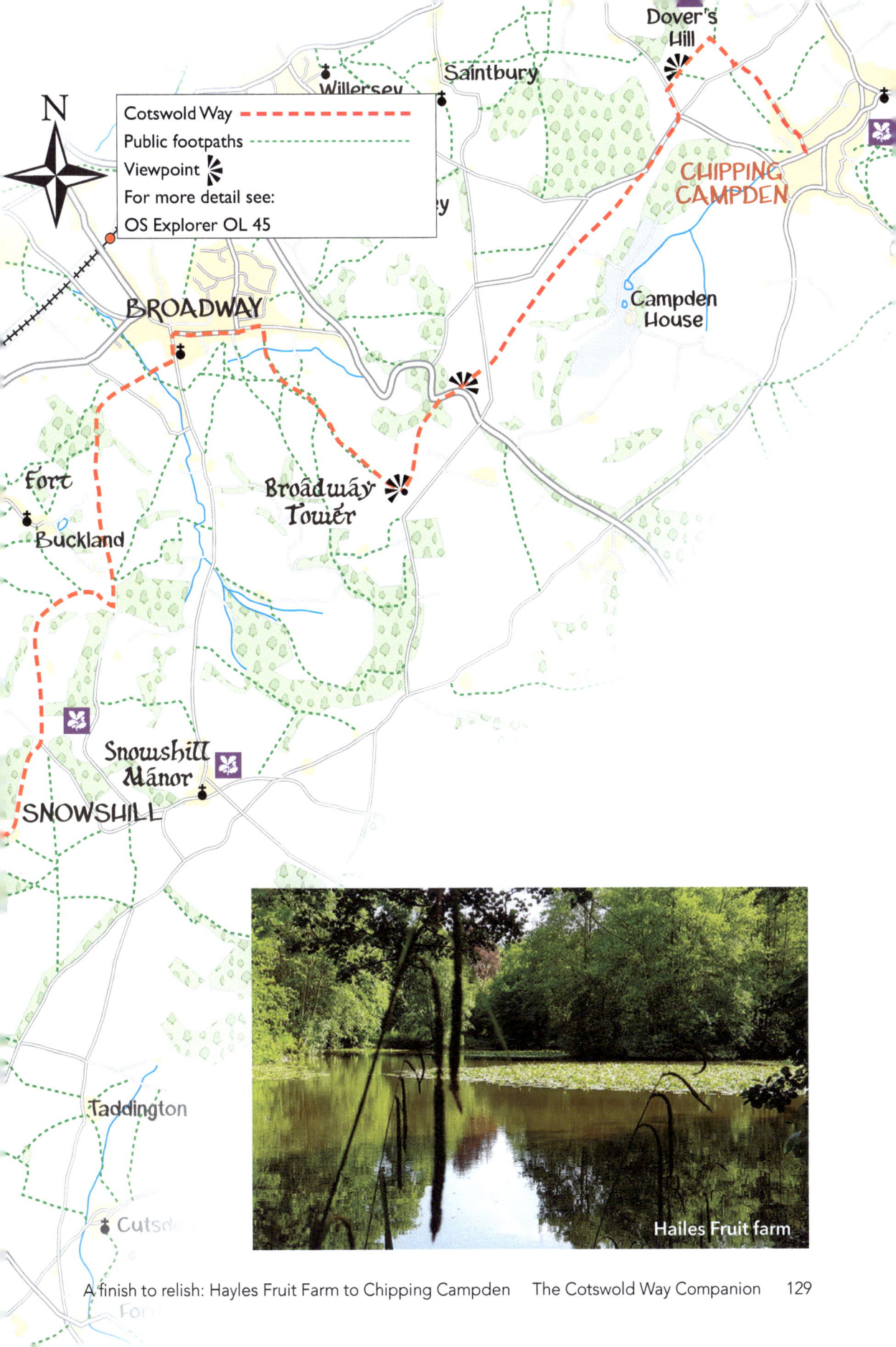

- Cotswold Way — — —
- Public footpaths - - - - -
- Viewpoint
- For more detail see:
- OS Explorer OL 45

N

Dover's Hill

Willersey

Saintbury

CHIPPING CAMPDEN

BROADWAY

Campden House

Fort

Buckland

Broadway Tower

Snowshill Manor

SNOWSHILL

Taddington

Cutsd...

Hailes Fruit farm

you look carefully closeby, you will see signs of a couple of bowl barrows: as Chapter 2 explained, these are funerary monuments dating to the late Bronze Age and earlier. They were constructed as earthen or rubble, sometimes ditched coverering single or multiple burials.

The Stanways

From Stumps Cross, the trail drops down to the Stanways with wonderful views across to Toddington and Bredon Hill in the distance. Wood Stanway comes first - it's a collection of houses including several large ones from the 17th and 18th centuries. Some go back earlier, however, as the reference to 'glebe' you'll see suggests - they belonged to Tewkesbury Abbey.

Shortly after, you will come to the cluster of buildings that is the estate village of Stanway, with its manor house, church and cottages that remain the property of the estate. Here you are in for some real treats. You've probably heard about the 'glory' of the Stanway water garden. Its centrepiece is the single-jet fountain. At 300ft (91+ metres) high, it's the tallest fountain in Britain, the tallest gravity fountain in the world and the second tallest fountain in Europe after Lake Geneva's turbine-driven one. Operated by remote control, and opened in 2004, it's driven by a reservoir 600 ft (183 metres) above, with water passing through a 12 inch poly pipe to a 2 inch nozzle.

Not so well known are the Stanway Estate's other treasures. First up is a fully restored working flour mill, re-opened by HRH The Prince of Wales in 2009. Its 24-foot (7.3 metre) overshot water wheel drives traditional cast-iron machinery and heavy burr-quartz millstones to produce stone ground flour from wheat grown close by on the estate: it was made by local iron-master, James Savory of Tewkesbury, around 1850.

After that is the Jacobean manor built in the 1630s and lived in by the same family since. Stanway House, which you might recognise as a set for the filming of Hilary Mantel's *Wolf Hall* books, was built around 1580 on the ruins of an earlier Tudor and even older house - the Abbey of Tewkesbury owned the manor from 715 AD. In 1533 the manor was purchased from the Abbey by Richard Tracy, and it

Manorway, Stanton

The Stanway Gatehouse

was his son Paul who began the present house. Now owned by the Earl of Wemyss, there are some wonderful gardens and an impressive tithe barn.

It's the gatehouse shown in the photograph above, however, which is the gem. Said to be one of the best pieces of architecture in the Cotswolds, it was built for Sir Richard Tracy in 1630. It is unusually positioned at right angles to the house, presumably because the church was in the way in front of the house. The lodges, either side of the gateway, have narrow bay windows and the whole is topped by shaped gables crowned with scallop shells that are the crest of the Tracy family. The archway has fluted columns on either side.

f you're knowledgeable about such things, you will appreciate that the scallop shell is also the crest of the apostle St James. He's the patron saint of pilgrims - and his shrine is in the cathedral of Santiago de Compostela in Galicia in northwestern Spain, where tradition holds his remains are buried. Making the crest especially famous is the walk known as the Camino de Santiago Compostela and the network of pilgrims' ways and trails leading to the shrine.

It's probably a coincidence that the scallop shell features in the Tracy family crest. But one of Thomas à Becket's four murderers in 1170 does happen to be from the Tracy family - he was William de Tracy. Subsequently, as well as being excommunicated by Pope Alexander, he and his fellow assassins were also required to make a pilgrimage to Rome, where the Pope reputedly ordered them to serve as knights in the Holy Lands for several years.

Walking from the gatehouse along the road, you pass St Peter's church built in the 12th century and, perhaps, over-restored by the Victorians. You round a corner, pass tennis courts on the left and come to the public entrance to the house on the right. Across to the left is the cricket pitch and a famous pavilion. Timber framed, and clad with larch poles, it sits on some twenty five mushroom-shaped staddle stones used to protect granaries and other similar buildings from vermin. J.M. Barrie, the creator of Peter Pan, is responsible for this. After the First World War, Barrie, who loved his cricket, was a regular guest at Stanway House. Indeed, as Wikipedia tells us, Barrie founded an amateur cricket team called the 'Allahakbarries' - under the mistaken belief that 'Allah akbar' meant 'Heaven help us' in Arabic rather than 'God is great'. Among the sometime players were Arthur Conan Doyle, H.G. Wells, Jerome K. Jerome, G. K. Chesterton, A. A. Milne, and P. G. Wodehouse.

Next stop Stanton

After the cricket pitch, you will be treated to a wonderful stretch of the trail, much of it tree-avenued, along the side of the escarpment. This takes you into your next place of exploration. It's Stanton. You have to see it to believe it. Surely, it must be in the running for the most quintessential village of the Cotswolds accolade if not 'the perfect Cotswold Village'. In Mark Richards' words:

There is an element of formality about the place derived, no doubt, from a desire to respect such bountiful beauty. The village is largely a 16th-century grouping of farmhouses and cottages growing very naturally in the mode of the time, yet somehow it has all worked out so well that the modern visitor cannot but admire the simple perfection of the place …

He goes on to talk about Stanton's rare architectural cohesion ...

Each house in turn bears its own distinct character without regimentation. The village is akin to the composition of a master painter who knows that if his work is to endure it must draw the spectator's eye on with mounting curiosity.

A Stott lantern in Stanton

Stanton, like other places on this stage, owes a great debt of gratitude to benefactors. In this case it was Sir Philip (Sidney) Stott, the architect, surveyor and civil engineer renowned across the globe for the design of cotton mills. By the end of the 19th Century, Stanton was pretty run down. Having accumulated his wealth largely from the shares he held in the mills he designed rather than fees, Stott purchased Stanton Court at the entrance to the village and much of the village besides (around 882 acres) in 1906. From then until his death in 1937, he spent much of his time and money restoring and revitalising the village and its community, including building a reservoir and bringing in lighting. You can still see Stott lanterns around the village. It was only In 1949 that his son decided to sell the estate (now 1330 acres).

You'll be pleased to know that, as the trail leaves the village and goes up to the escarpment at Shenberrow Hill Fort, it passes the Mount Inn, one of the eighteen Donnington pubs in the north Cotswolds owned by the Arkle family. Enjoy one of the local ales - Donnington brewery is not far away near Stow - along with views, and make plans to walk the Donnington Way some time: it runs from Willersey just north of Broadway down to the Fox Inn at Great Barrington near Burford in the south.

If you have the time, make an ever so slight detour to the Stanton Guildhouse up the lane. Mary Osborne was responsible for this. The story goes that, working at a centre for the poor in London's East End, she met Mahatma Gandhi who impressed her with his descriptions of simple religious retreats - 'ashrams' - he had founded in India. So she set up a charitable trust and set about building a centre to rekindle and nurture country crafts and skills, together with the many forms of artistic expression from painting to musical appreciation. The building, which used reclaimed materials from the surrounding area, paving stones from the streets of London and oak from the Blenheim Palace estate, was completed in 1973 with the help of young international volunteers and local people. It's still in operation and seeks to fulfil the mission Mary Osborne gave it.

Along and over the escarpment into Broadway

Leaving Stanton, the trail continues along the side of the escarpment passing Laverton and Buckland on your left. It then goes up and over the escarpment going down into Broadway. Often referred to as the 'Jewel of the Cotswolds', Broadway lies in Worcestershire. As Broadway History Society explains, it was originally centred around the old church of St Eadburgha to the right of the map before gradually expanding northwards. Its current wide main street reflects the fact that two small streams ran through the village; people built on either side of the streams and a road formed down the middle. In the winter, the mud from this 'Broadway' piled up and in the summer grass grew on the piles accounting for today's verges.

As in other Cotswold towns, initial growth and wealth was based on the wool and cloth trade. Also very important, however, was that in the 1500s, a route from Worcester to Oxford and London over Fish Hill was built and the White Hart (now the Lygon Arms) was established shortly afterwards. Broadway became a busy stagecoach stop on the Worcester to London route providing all the services needed, including grooms and extra horses for the steep haul up Fish Hill. At one time, there were as many as 33 public houses. There aren't as many today, but enough for you to enjoy. The road between Evesham and the top of Fish Hill became a toll-road as a result of legislation dated 1728. Tolls were collected at Turnpike House to be found in the upper High Street.

Key to the next stage of development was the coming of the railways in the mid-1900s, which stripped Broadway of its staging post role to make it something of a backwater. The upside was that many Victorian artists, composers and writers were drawn to its calm. As Chapter 2 has already pointed out, they included Elgar, John Singer Sargent, Edwin Austin Abbey, J. M. Barrie, Vaughan Williams, William Morris, Mary Anderson and American artist and writer, Francis Davis Millet. The furniture designer Gordon Russell grew up in Broadway and had a workshop here.

Look out for the seventeenth-century Farnham House on the village green - it was the unofficial first home of the Broadway group of artists sponsored by Mary Anderson. If you have the time, also visit the independent Ashmolean Museum. This was opened in Sept 2013 and is based in 'Tudor House' on the High Street. Originally built in the seventeenth century as a coaching inn, the house has been extended and adapted over the centuries, serving at various periods as part of a school, a farm, and a private residence for various owners,

To the Tower

Prepare yourself for a climb up to Broadway Tower. As you do, notice the dry stone walling on your left. It's on land owned by Broadway Trust and much of it is the handiwork of the Cotswold Wardens from the North District. Broadway Tower may only be about 20 metres high, but it's 312 metres above sea level and the second-highest point of the Cotswolds (after Cleeve Hill). It started life as a folly - the brainchild of Capability Brown and designed by James Wyatt in the form of a 'Saxon' castle. It was built in 1798–1799 for Lady Coventry who wanted to know whether a beacon on this hill could be seen from her house in Worcester about 22 miles (6.7 kms) away. You could. On a clear day, it's also claimed, you should have unrivalled views across a 62 miles or 100 kilometres radius and sixteen counties.

After being home to the printing press of Sir Thomas Phillipps in the mid-1800s, the tower was rented by Cormell Price, a close friend of artists William Morris, Edward Burne-Jones, and Dante Gabriel Rossetti. All three spent time living there in the 1880s.

In the late 1950s, the site of the Tower became home to an underground Royal Observer Corps Nuclear Bunker for monitoring fallout in the event of the 'cold war' becoming the real thing. Manned continuously from 1961, it was only stood down in 1991. The bunker is one of the few remaining fully equipped facilities in England; it's normally open at weekends and on Bank Holiday Mondays, subject to a small entrance fee.

As Wikipedia explains, between 1955 and 1991, more than 1,500 of these underground facilities were located across the UK, roughly ten miles apart, mainly in remote rural locations. They were of a standard design and constructed of twelve inch thick, steel-reinforced concrete twenty feet beneath the ground. In the event of a nuclear attack, these posts would have been manned by three members of the Royal Observer Corps (ROC). Their role would have been to note the details of a nuclear burst to be used by government and local authorities to decide how best to protect civilian life.

These bunkers had no mains water, electricity, gas, or heating. The only communication with the outside world was by way of a simple Tele-Talk system to headquarters and three to four other nearby ROC posts in the 'cluster group'. Needless to say, had these bunkers been used in an attack, conditions inside would have been rather uncomfortable.

Also near the tower is a memorial to the crew of an A.W.38 Whitley bomber. Sadly, it crashed there during a training mission in June 1943.

Via Dover's Hill to Chipping Campden

You're now on the final leg of the walk, which will take you into Chipping Campden, where the Cotswold Way ends. The trail takes you past Fish Hill, where there once was an inn of the same name, and onto what is known as The Mile Drive. As well as views of St James, look out for a small copse just off the road on your left. This is known as Martin's copse and is the final resting place of one of the original Cotswold Warden's stalwarts from Chipping Campden (Reg Martin) with the same name.

Further on, and not long before you approach Dover's Hill, look out on your left for the 'Kiftsgate Hundred' stone on the edge of Weston Park. As the name suggests, this marks the boundary of the local 'hundred'. In Anglo-Saxon times, a 'hundred' was the division of a shire for administrative, military and judicial purposes under the common law. Until the introduction of districts by the Local Government Act 1894, 'hundreds' were the only widely used administrative unit intermediate between the parish and the county in size.

One thing you must do is stop to take in the views from Dover's Hill now owned by the National Trust. On the top of the hill is a trig point together with a toposcope illustrating many of the landmarks that are visible from it. These include the Black Mountains in South Wales and the Long Mynd in Shropshire nearly 60 miles (97 kms) away.

The hill looks like an amphitheatre and, as Chipping Campden History Society tells us, is named after Robert Dover an English attorney, author and wit born towards the end of the 1500s. In 1611 he moved to live close by in Saintbury and set about inaugurating an annual Cotswold Olimpick Games on the hill in about 1612, presiding over them for forty years.

A mixture of courtly and folk events, the Cotswold Olimpicks, so named in *Annalia Dubrensia*, one of a series of literary celebrations of the events, consisted of cudgel-playing, wrestling, running at the quintain, jumping, casting the bar and hammer, hand-ball, gymnastics, rural dances and games and horse-racing, the winners in which received valuable prizes.

The Games were interrupted by the outbreak of the English Civil War, revived after the Restoration, and continued until 1852, when the land was partitioned between farmers and landowners as part of the Enclosures Act. There was a one-off revival in 1951 for the Festival of Britain, but it was only with establishment of The Robert Dover's Games Society in 1965 that the event became a fixture again.

The trig point on Dover's Hill

These days the Cotswolds Olimpicks are held on the Friday after Spring Bank Holiday. Their very existence came in particularly useful to the British Olympic Association in its successful bid for the 2012 Olympic Games in London. Dover's games, it said, were proof positive of 'the first stirrings of Britain's Olympic beginnings'.

To mark the end of the games, there is a bonfire and firework display, followed by a torch-lit procession back into the town and dancing in the square. The Scuttlebrook Wake takes place the following day. The locals don fancy dress costumes and follow the Scuttlebrook Queen, with her four attendants and Page Boy, in a procession to the centre of town pulled on a decorated dray by the town's own Morris Men. This is then followed by the presentation of prizes and displays of Maypole dancing by the two primary schools and Morris dancing.

That the hill is in National Trust hands is largely down to another benefactor featured in Chipping Campden History Society's archives: Frederick Griggs - a renowned etcher and architect. Attracted by Chipping Campden's outstanding architectural heritage, beautiful surroundings and living tradition of craftsmanship, Griggs settled in Chipping Campden in 1904. Over the next 25 years, he devoted his resources and energies to protecting its heritage and charm.

The story goes that in 1926, the then owner of Dover's Hill was obliged to sell the land by auction. An attempt to raise the money before the sale produced only £700, so Griggs decided to risk everything and buy the hill himself. His bid of £4,400 for the 178 acres was successful. After the sale, Griggs attempted what today would be called 'crowdfunding', posting a letter from the National Trust in The Times appealing for help. The hoped-for support was slow in coming, however, and two days before Christmas Griggs was obliged to write a personal cheque for £2,000 with friends finding the balance.

Chipping Campden - the market town built on wool

Just two words give you the key to unlocking Chipping Campden's secrets. One is in the name. 'Chipping' is Old English for 'market'. The town's first market charter was awarded in 1180, with the 'Chipping' prefix becoming popular by the middle of the 1200s. Blessed by its position close to the Fosse Way on the old trade route to Cirencester, Chipping Campden became the focus of an expanding area. A key figure was Hugh de Gondeville, who Mark Richards describes as the 'effective founder' of the famous curved marketplace, where you will find the Cotswold Way 'end / beginning' stone. de Gondeville, it seems, was asked to take over the manor in 1185 on behalf of Henry II. It was de Gondeville who developed the township by laying out a market street on a new open site.

According to the Chipping Campden History Society, de Gondeville has in the past been identified as one of the knights, along with William de Tracy mentioned earlier, who murdered Thomas à Becket in 1170. However, it is now considered that this is incorrect. At that time, at least three knights were known by that name, including one who was Sheriff of a county and another who was tutor to one of the king's sons.

The other word that goes with Chipping Campden is 'wool'. In the two centuries after 1066, there was a significant shift in emphasis across the Cotswolds from arable to pasture farming, with sheep making an indelible impression. The Cotswolds became internationally renowned for its wool and Chipping Campden one of the major centres for its trade, with merchant families emerging and trading large quantities from Wales and Marches with Italy and Spain as well as the Low countries.

The buildings in the High Street so celebrated by Pevsner, the old grammar school and St James' church and the mini cathedral that is St James', reflect a bygone era when the rich invested much of their wealth into the local community, helping to make the landscape and environment what it is today. One such was William Grevel whose house, shown in the drawing below, was built in the 1300s.

The decline of the wool trade in 15 century as a result of the wars with France ushered in a period of relative decline for Chipping Campden. Unlike Wotton, Dursley and Painswick, making cloth wasn't a serious option because of the lack of streams and rivers to drive the wheels of mills. Yet the landscape and its environment had become such that admirers effectively came to the rescue. There was some great re-building in the late 1500s, followed by significant civic endowment developments associated with Sir Baptist Hicks in the first half of the 1600s - Hicks was a close confidant of James 1 and effectively one of his bankers. It was at this time that the Almshouses and Woolstaplers Hall were built, along with Campden House. Sadly, the latter was burnt down during the English Civil War just some thirty years later and all that now remains are two gatehouses, two Jacobean banqueting houses, restored by the Landmark Trust and Lady Juliana's gateway. Hick's descendants still live at the Court House attached to the site.

St James - resplendent 'wool' church

It's also because of its landscape and environment that Chipping Campden and the area more generally came to be associated with the arts and craft movement. It was C.R. Ashbee who brought the 'Guild and School of Handicraft' to Campden in 1902. Ashbee established these in 1888 in London, while a resident at Toynbee Hall, one of the original settlements set up to alleviate inner city poverty in Whitechapel; it was housed in workshops at Essex House, Mile End Road, with a retail outlet in the heart of the West End in fashionable Mayfair. The School closed in 1895 with Ashbee, according to Wikipedia, blaming 'the failure of the Technical Education Board of the London County Council to keep its word … and the impossibility of carrying on costly educational work in the teeth of state aided competition'.

The closeby Court Barn is now a museum celebrating the rich Arts and Crafts tradition of the area. The permanent display celebrates nine lives or workshops that were established in the north Cotswolds.

It starts with C.R. Ashbee and then continues with former members of Ashbee's Guild who remained working in Chipping Campden following its dissolution in 1908:

- Alec Miller (wood carver & sculptor)
- the Hart family (silversmiths).
- Gordon Russell (furniture)
- Katharine Adams (bookbinding)
- Paul Woodroffe (stained glass & book illustration)
- F.L. Griggs (etching & engraving)
- Michael Cardew (Winchcombe Pottery)
- Robert Welch (silversmith & product designer)

It survived only until 1907, but added another phase to the town's landmarks and character. One legacy is the silk mill in Sheep Street in the centre - still home to the Hart family silversmiths. Another, indirectly, is the Court Barn Museum.

Grevel House

Cotswold Way Circular Walks

This final leg of the Cotswold Way offers up no fewer than three of the Cotswold Way Circular walks. First up, assuming you're walking the south-north route, is Stanton, Snowshill and the Edge. As the title suggests, this walk enables you to take in not just Stanton but also Snowshill - for many, a village with a strong claim to the title of the most picturesque villages in the Cotswolds.

It also means you can go up and over the scarp to take in views in different directions. You can extend your day out with a visit to the National Trust's Snowshill Manor, which you will pass on route. Here you will find yet more features of the arts and craft movement's activities. You can also stop off at the Snowshill Arms - another Donnington pub on the walk of the same name. It's particularly well-known for the menu's offering of a cup of chips - which means you can have your chips without feeling too guilty!

The second walk is described as Broadway and the Tower. If you want the challenge, go up to the tower directly from Broadway on the Cotswold Way. If you prefer a slightly gentler elevation, go from Broadway via St Eadburgha's church, which was where Broadway first started. Either way, you won't be disappointed. This enchanting walk leads you through the picturesque Cotswold high street of Broadway, along historic tracks and up to the intriguing Broadway Tower with its spectacular views across the Severn Vale into Wales.

The third walk is described as Chipping Campden and Dover's Hill. In this case you have the choice of starting in Chipping Campden itself or on Dover's Hill. If you start on Dover's Hill, you also have the slightly shorter three mile option avoiding the climb up and down to the town. Go in May and you'll catch the bluebells in Lynches Wood.

- You can download the maps for these walks from www.nationaltrail.co.uk

Car Parking

- For the start from Hayles Fruit Farm, see the end point on the previous stage.

- In Chipping Campden, you can try the Market Square car park in the famous High Street (GL55 6AW) and, in school holidays, Chipping Campden School, which is close by. Sheep Street and Back Ends (yes, there is one!) are other possibilities.

- If you want to break your walk on this stage, parking is difficult in Stanway. Stanton, however, has a small public car park at the village hall (WR12 7NG). There are also two long stay car parks in Broadway: Milestone Ground (WR12 7HA) and Shear House (WR12 7ET). Fish Hill (WR12 7LB) and Dover's Hill (GL55 6UW) are also possibilities.